LET US BLESS THE LORD ^{YEAR ONE}

Meditations on the Daily Office

ADVENT THROUGH HOLY WEEK

Volume 1

Barbara Cawthorne Crafton

MOREHOUSE PUBLISHING
A Continuum imprint
HARRISBURG • LONDON • NEW YORK

Morehouse Publishing, P.O. Box 1321, Harrisburg, PA 17105

Morehouse Publishing, The Tower Building, 11 York Road, London SE1 7NX

Morehouse Publishing is a Continuum imprint.

Unless otherwise indicated, biblical quotations are from the New Revised Standard Version Bible, copyright 1989, Division of Christian Education of the National Council of the Churches of Christ in the United States of America. Used by permission. All rights reserved.

Cover art: Shaffer/Smith/SuperStock

Cover design: Laurie Westhafer

Library of Congress Cataloging-in-Publication Data

Crafton, Barbara Cawthorne.
    Let us bless the Lord. Year one : meditations on the Daily Office / Barbara Cawthorne Crafton.
      p.   cm.
    ISBN 0-8192-1982-7 (hardcover)
    1. Devotional calendars—Episcopal Church. 2. Bible—Meditations.
3. Divine office. 4. Episcopal Church—Prayer-books and devotions—English.
I. Title.
BV4812.C73   2004
242'.3—dc22

                         2004006016

Printed in the United States of America

04 05 06 07 08 09   10 9 8 7 6 5 4 3 2 1

CONTENTS

INTRODUCTION

We were the early risers in the family, my father and I. I would hear him first, from upstairs in my room: the clatter of the teakettle and teacups. I would put on my sneakers without any socks, pull my red jacket over my pajamas and go downstairs. We would go outside then, to look at the garden, he with his hoe, I with only my eyes and ears. We made the circuit of the vegetables and flowers: "Beans are coming," he would say, and poke around the roots of a plant with the hoe. I would nod, happy just to be with him, walking carefully around the edge of the garden, feeling the delicious squish of water that had soaked my sneakers through. The plants were different each day: more leaves, taller, a deeper green as time went on, the little flowers, the tiny fruit.

After the tour of the garden, we went inside. Soon the fragrant tea filled the china cups, and slices of toast were ready for their coats of orange marmalade. The clink of cutlery against china was the only sound; my father and I were not talkative. Besides, he was busy with his stack of books that sat next to his chair: his prayer book, his Bible, his book of daily meditations. He was in prayer while we ate our breakfast. He was reading the same service of Morning Prayer that I now read. The sameness of everything anchored me comfortably then. It anchors me still.

Later, in seminary, the same: Morning Prayer with the same people every day, Evening Prayer sung with beauty and dignity, linking the love of learning with the loveliness of music and text in a marriage that has lasted longer than many. We sat in rows in the chapel choir, a thousand doubts about our futures, about our ability, about our worthiness—all silenced, for a moment, in the beauty of holiness. *O, God make speed to save us,* we sang. *O Lord , make haste to help us.* Over the following decades we were saved and helped. Oh, yes. Many times.

Sunday evenings at St. Clement's in Hell's Kitchen: For the first several years, we were in the shabby parish hall around a long table, crooked candles in a motley assortment of holders lighting our prayer books. Old and young, homeless and housed, crazy and nominally sane, we gathered for that same helping and saving. It was easy to teach this assortment of beloved oddballs the ancient words and plainsong tunes. Back and forth we went in the old way, *Phos hilaron* and *Magnificat* and *Nunc dimittis. Let us bless the Lord,* I would sing at the end, and they would sing back to me, *Thanks be to God.* I sing it myself, now, often, when I am alone, and I see and hear them again. How I miss them! I can weep thinking about them. *They only come for the meal afterward,* some people said. And it was true that many of them needed the meal. But they all could have gotten it without coming to prayer. They needed the prayer as well.

Later on, we had a beautiful new chapel. Stained glass windows. New chairs. New organ. A fine altar. Perfect lighting. The evening sun slanted through the windows. Sometimes the clip-clop of a horse's hooves sounded outside; the city's livery stables were down the street from St. Clement's. Now we sat on our new chairs and held our new prayer books, lit the new candles in their elegant new candlesticks. But we were the same, me and my congregation: still funny, the crazy still crazy, the frail a little frailer, all of us a little older.

Now I read the Daily Office in my office at home. Its paneled walls are soft yellow, with sheer white curtains at the window and tall shelves of books. I have a wonderful Office Book, containing all the readings and all the psalms and all the collects and the services for morning, noon, evening, and compline. All in one book. No more juggling Bibles. Or sometimes I use the service at www.missionstclare.com. No juggling there, either.

When I finish Morning Prayer, I send an e-mail to a few hundred friends who have banded together to pray, each of us in his or her own place, at his or her own time. *Let us bless the Lord,* I type, and press "send." Into the mysterious ether it flies, and soon the answers begin to appear in my inbox. *Thanks be to God,* says one after another. And my dad. And my seminary classmates, living and dead. And the Fathers of the Church, and its forgotten Mothers. And now, you. *Thanks be to God.*

BCC
The Geranium Farm
2004

Advent

SUNDAY, ADVENT I

Pss 146, 147 * 111, 112, 113
Isaiah 1:1–9
2 Peter 3:1–10
Matthew 25:1–13

But the day of the Lord will come like a thief,
and then the heavens will pass away . . .
2 PETER 3:10

Do you think it's working? The compost pile has settled a bit in the past week or so, down about five inches from where it was. *I think so,* my husband Q says. *We'll see after the first few snows. Sometimes it works so hard it will melt the snow. If you poke a hole in it, it steams.*

Wow. Microscopic life changing with such feverishness that it throws off heat. Enough to melt snow. Earthworms charging through the warm darkness, receiving and discharging the stuff of life, reducing everything they eat to velvety black granules. Roots of unwanted plants take advantage of the warmth and twine their way throughout the pile, storing enough in their pale stems to burst into green life at the first hint of sunlight. The living and dying just below the surface of the snow is the generation of life itself—leave a couple of earthworms alone together in the compost pile in the fall, and it will be full of them come spring. Creating food for the plants, they also create themselves, over and over again.

Apart from the biology of us—our bodies do exactly the same thing theirs do—our living and dying causes new life to spring forth in other ways. We plumb an idea or a practice to its depths and then find it inadequate, unable to accompany us further, and so we set it aside. But its rejected skeleton is the scaffold upon which we erect the next edifice of our striving. One day, that, too, will be unable to sustain us. And so it goes.

Our cultures, governments, nations, economic systems, all our institutions—they are temporary. Our descendents will outstrip them. We fight against the very thought of our obsolescence, but it is so. There is nothing on earth that does not seed future life with its own death.

MONDAY IN ADVENT I

Pss 1, 2, 3 * 4, 7
Isaiah 1:10–20
1 Thessalonians 1:1–10
Luke 20:1–8

I do not delight in the blood of bulls . . .
ISAIAH 1:11

It must have been a terrible shock to every single person in Israel when the temple was destroyed. It happened twice: once when the Israelites were conquered by the Babylonians and led off in captivity, after which it was rebuilt, and then again in the first century CE, when Rome finally lost patience with them. Razed to the ground both times. Its only remains now are called the "wailing wall"—people write out their prayers on little pieces of paper and leave them there, pushed into the cracks between the stones. I have heard that you can fax and e-mail them in now, if you're not in Jerusalem yourself.

Shock though it was, both times, this passage from Isaiah shows us that people in Israel had always understood the majesty of God to transcend even the worship of the temple cult. At the height of the sacrifice of animals as the central act of Jewish worship, people always knew that it was no substitute for a lively and committed life of obedience to the holy will of God. No outward practice could conceal an inner rot.

It was a good thing they understood this, for the time would come when they would leave the temple behind forever. No sacrifices would be possible according to the rules set forth in Leviticus, not ever again. It was a good thing that they learned how to be faith-

ADVENT

ful without that building in that city, for they would be scattered to the four corners of the earth. Most of them, and most of their descendents, would never see it again.

The destruction of the temple, that great tragedy in Jewish memory, set Judaism free, free to become the majestic heritage of law and ethics we know it as today. A cult centered around temple sacrifice could never have survived the Holocaust—it would never have lasted into modern times.

Sometimes losing something very important plunges us into the deep end of God's mysterious will. And there we find—sometimes—that there is much more for us than we would ever have thought possible, had it not been for that very loss.

TUESDAY IN ADVENT I

Pss 5, 6 * 10, 11
Isaiah 1:21–31
1 Thessalonians 2:1–12
Luke 20:9–18

Ah, I will pour out my wrath on my enemies . . .
ISAIAH 1:24

I thought a "blizzard" was a type of monster when I was little. A blizzard was coming, I was told, and so we all needed to stay inside. It sounded too much like "lizard" to be anything but a Godzilla-style predator. I wondered why we didn't make a break for it before it came, but my parents knew best, I supposed. It wouldn't do to begin our getaway in the car, only to have the blizzard pursue us down the street, catching our Plymouth easily up in one taloned forepaw and biting it in half as we sat screaming inside.

Why was the blizzard coming, I asked my grandmother. Oh, it's the season for them, she said, seeming unafraid. The monster had a regular season, then. What had made my parents decide to settle in such a dangerous part of the world? A place with a blizzard season, a place to which the terrible creatures returned annually, like the swallows to Capistrano?

All these conclusions of mine made a certain sense. Kids' reasoning is like that: If you accept their starting premise, you can usually grasp how they end up where they do. We base our hope or fear of the future on what we know from the past. It's all we have to work with.

And so we react with suspicion when something truly new happens. When God acts in a way unlike the ways in which we have seen God act, we're not sure it's God. Maybe it's a giant, destroying lizard.

Stay in your house. Keep your post by the window and keep warm. Look at what descends from the new thing. But look at every aspect of it and not just at the parts you can behold without fear.

WEDNESDAY IN ADVENT I

Pss 119:1–24 * 12, 13, 14
Isaiah 2:1–11
1 Thessalonians 2:13–20
Luke 20:19–26

The haughty eyes of people shall be brought low,
and the pride of everyone shall be humbled . . .
ISAIAH 2:11

The subway doors open and two men get on, carrying a long roll of carpet together. The train is mercifully uncrowded, and they maneuver their awkward load onto a bench. Then they sit on the roll. At Times Square, they edge it back out the door, hoist it onto their shoulders and march it toward the turnstiles.

I haven't seen that in a while, James said. I nodded. *I took a huge bookcase on the subway once.* Whatever you can fit into a subway car, you can move. It's a great city.

Two people carrying something long and heavy have to communicate. Instinctively, I yield to Q in all of our portage: It is best if one mind directs such a delicate business, not two. Not if one of the minds is as stubborn as my mind.

Such times are not optimal for contests about who gets his way. Some things simply cannot be can be accomplished by consensus and carrying a ladder is one of them. Sometimes you just need a director. He may or may not be smarter than you, and for the task at hand, that doesn't matter. But he is still the director.

Moving gracefully in and out of positions of power is a mark of spiritual maturity. If you can only be the boss, or if you never can, there's a piece missing. In a way, it's the same piece—people have gifts and the power to deploy them. Their gifts rise to the top, as needed. It is not vain or ruthless to trust in them. It is not craven to submit to them. You just do what works best.

THURSDAY IN ADVENT I

Pss 18:1–20 * 18:21–50
Isaiah 2:12–22
1 Thessalonians 3:1–13
Luke 20:27–40

Indeed they cannot die any more, because they are like angels and are children of God, being children of the resurrection.
LUKE 20:36

A fire in the fireplace. Two votive candles that have "Peace on Earth" etched on their sides so that the light shines through the letters. Another candle, red and smelling of cinnamon, set in a ring of red berries. National Public Radio's "All Things Considered" on the radio. Furry slippers and a furry cat. A cup of tea.

This is what heaven must be like in the winter.

But in heaven, there is no great gulf of deprivation against which I may rejoice in my blessings. An even stream of joy obtains there, and I know that I—as I am now constituted—would not tolerate it for long.

But we won't *be* as we are. We shall be changed, built at last to live the life God lives without dying of it. Ancient texts reveal that the biblical writers thought human beings incapable of looking directly upon God and surviving. *Humankind cannot bear very much reality,* is how T. S. Eliot put it, and we know what he meant.

For Paul, this is unqualified good news. He can hardly wait. We are not so sure we want to be so changed, though, not at all sure that the thought of those we have loved and lost being so other than as we remember them is good news at all. Don't they miss us? Aren't they sad, to see us so sad?

And them? What do they say? *Don't they see us? Don't they see how lovely it is? Can't they see what is all around them? How can they not see?*

But we don't. Not yet. Heaven is in our imagination, and sometimes we think it is only there. That it's a story. A lie, even. And it *is* a story. That business about its streets being paved with gold—don't count on it. But you can count on what's important about it: God is there. All flesh is there, changed and glorified. We can count on that.

FRIDAY IN ADVENT I

Pss 16, 17 * 22
Isaiah 3:8–15
1 Thessalonians 4:1–12
Luke 20:41–21:4

What do you mean by crushing my people,
by grinding the face of the poor?
ISAIAH 3:15

I feel enormous—I didn't overeat at the Thanksgiving table per se, but I nibbled all day preparing the meal. I had pumpkin pie for breakfast the next day, two pieces of it, telling myself something dishonest about the beta-carotene it contained.

And so it's back to the gym today. It is full of women, pushing and pulling, kicking, twisting, trotting, and marching away on the little wooden platforms. You can barely find a place to join in the circuit. I guess we all feel enormous. But we all also feel better for being there: Maybe we're enormous, but at least we're moving.

How strange all this is: Americans' worst health problem is obesity, while half the world goes to bed hungry every night. Couldn't we equalize things a little, send our excess to where it's needed? Honor our bodies while restoring theirs? I have dreamed of this all my life, dreamed that my self-absorbed discontent with my figure could be turned to some good.

Is it true that we will always have the poor with us? Necessary and true? That, no matter how smart we get, we will never bridge the gap between have and have-not? That some of us will always fret about our cellulite while some of us will poke through garbage, looking for food? It was that way in biblical times. Hardly anything is now as it was then, but this is: There are still two worlds, the world of plenty and the world of not enough. Will it always be so?

Then, as now, it is a matter of our hearts. It isn't necessary. It's a choice. We chose to have it so. The people in the Bible had a hard time seeing this, and we do, too. We shake our heads and mutter something fatalistic about life being hard. It's hard, all right.

But it's much harder for some of us than for others. You and me, for instance. You can read and I can write. Worldwide, that puts us in the top half.

Lord, have mercy.

SATURDAY IN ADVENT I

Pss 20, 21:1–7 (8–14) * 110:1–5 (6–7), 116, 117
Isaiah 4:2–6
1 Thessalonians 4:13–18
Luke 21:5–19

*We do not want you to be uninformed, brothers and
sisters, about those who have died, so that you
may not grieve as others do who have no hope.*

1 THESSALONIANS 4:13

Don't forget to light a candle. I'm on my way to the city, and Q is staying home.

I won't. He won't forget: one for his son Ross and one for my stillborn baby. Candles for children who have died, long before their time. No matter how long ago, no matter what the cause.

This will be our second candle-lighting of the day. The Compassionate Friends held one this afternoon. There were sad little poems, a mother sang a song, and then we all lit candles for the children we have lost. Most parents said a few words as they placed the candle in front of the picture they had brought: little shrines. Q and I brought holly and poinsettias. People brought food. It was nice.

Such pain in that room: It is as if it were a room full of quadruple amputees. Why on earth are we alive and here, when such a thing has happened? Why not take us? Such bargaining arrests the occasional freakish moment but, for the most part, the people here are used to it: Grief is conjoined to them forevermore, and in spite of it they have learned to live. And, for the most part, to live well.

The grace given us under impossible circumstances is miraculous. *How're you doing?* One man asks another as they drink coffee from paper cups. *I'm here,* he says, and the other dad puts a quiet hand on his shoulder. Nothing more need be said. Nothing more to say.

Many of them feel that any strength they have comes from the children they have lost. Most of them feel that their children are in another place, looking after them in another way. Most of them haven't a clue as to what that place is, or how their children live in it. Most of them wait for it longingly, and light a candle.

SUNDAY, ADVENT II

Pss 148, 149, 150 * 114, 115
Isaiah 5:1–7
2 Peter 3:11–18
Luke 7:28–35

Let me sing for my beloved my love-song . . .
ISAIAH 5:1

I plunge my foot up to the ankle into a puddle of freezing water. Why didn't I wear my boots? The snow, as promised, has turned to sleety rain, and every patch of white disguises a small icy river.

Q will stay home tonight, while I preach the sermon at a Dignity Mass. Dignity is the organization of gay and lesbian Roman Catholics and their friends. The New York chapter meets every Sunday evening for a mass and fellowship afterward.

These masses have a sweet, sweet spirit. It is not possible for the members to be open about the whole of who they are, in almost all of their parishes. This may not sound like much to many people, who are apt to say something like *Well, why should we be focused on sex at all in church*?

But that's not really it. It's not that gay and lesbian people want every conversation to be a sexual one, any more than straight people do. They just want to be allowed to be safely who they are. I sit beside my husband at a church supper and absently massage the middle of his back: I know he gets stiff and sore there sometimes. He touches my back with one hand as we walk up the aisle of a theater after a play. We both wear gold rings to show the world we belong to each other. We don't think of sex all the time. But we are who we are, and we would miss our casual physicality if it were denied us.

Sex isn't everything. But it's part of being human. Like love and friendship. And faith.

MONDAY IN ADVENT II

Pss 25 * 9, 15
Isaiah 5:8–12, 18–23
1 Thessalonians 5:1–11
Luke 21:20–28

People will faint from fear and foreboding of what is coming
upon the world, for the powers of the heavens will be shaken.
LUKE 21:26

That's an unbelievable wind out there, Q said as he hung up his hat and scarf. I'll say. I had been watching the tall old pine tree outside my office window sway crazily back and forth, as if it were a sapling. I had, just the other day, argued for its removal and lost. Now I wondered if it might not crash through the roof and kill me.

Then I would be numbered among the small but interesting population of people who are killed by freak natural disasters when sitting in their own houses, minding their own business.

Jesus thinks of them, those unexpected victims of whimsical chance, those wrong-place-at-the-wrong-time people. It will come suddenly, he says. You won't see it coming.

Stay ready, because you don't know when. Something mighty will come and change your life in an instant.

Maybe something bad, but maybe something good. The coming of the messiah is unexpected, too, like a tree falling on your house, only life-giving, not death-dealing: right place at the right time. Prepare your whole life: You will still be shocked when it happens to you. Expect Christ from childhood—you will still be amazed at his goodness. Familiarity seems not to get in his way—read a passage from scripture for the thousandth time, and suddenly see something you could swear was not there before. Hear the story of the circumstances surrounding his birth yet again, and find something brand new in them.

Christ is new to us because each moment is new to us. We are so changeable, so tossed about by the winds of change. Never exactly the same two days in a row. And Christ is ready for us, in whatever shape we stumble toward him. Now it's time for us to get ready.

TUESDAY IN ADVENT II

Pss 26, 28 * 36, 39
Isaiah 5:13–17, 24–25
1 Thessalonians 5:12–28
Luke 21:29–38

Be on guard so that your hearts are not weighed down with dissipation and drunkenness and the worries of this life, and that day does not catch you unexpectedly, like a trap. For it will come upon all who live on the face of the whole earth.

LUKE 21:34–35

We've all got to go sometime. None of us are getting out of here alive. Many, many people think it's in very poor taste to mention that fact, that it's morbid to think about it. Many, many people truly feel that the best way to go through life is never to think about death. *It'll just depress me,* they tell themselves. *Best to put it out of my mind.*

I just haven't found that to be the case. I have found, rather, that thinking about the end of my life makes me want to use the time I have left to the fullest. That it makes me think of heaven and what it must be like, of my purpose here on earth. That it reminds me of those I have loved who have gone before me, and of the great blessing they were in my life, greater blessings than I ever realized while they still lived. Thinking of death helps me value life. And it helps me not to be afraid.

American life is all about insulating ourselves from our mortality. We must be constantly amused, diverted, we must flit from one thing to another, never allowing ourselves to come to a gentle stop and ponder exactly where we are and where we want to go. Everything is supposed to be easy, and we are to view things that aren't easy for us as an outrage. Everything is supposed to be fast, and we're not supposed to have to wait for anything. Everyone is supposed to stay young and beautiful forever. We must walk into our houses and immediately turn on the television, lest we hear something eternal in our silence. Silence makes us nervous because of what we might hear.

What we might hear is the voice of God. *Don't be afraid. I am here, and I will stay with you until it is time for you to come to me, and that will be a wonderful thing.*

WEDNESDAY IN ADVENT II

Pss 38 * 119:25–48
Isaiah 6:1–13
2 Thessalonians 1:1–12
John 7:53–8:11

. . . for I am a man of unclean lips, and I live among a people of unclean lips; yet my eyes have seen the King, the Lord of hosts!
ISAIAH 6:5

For a moment, Isaiah is filled with despair: He is not up to this. He is not up to what has happened. He is not worthy, and he knows it.

But he doesn't stay that way. His remarkable vision continues, and the cleansing glory of God surrounds him with such vividness and power that he quite forgets about his own uncleanness. Suddenly, it's not about him anymore. Suddenly, it is not his worthiness or virtue or power that is being called forth. Suddenly, it's all about God, and God has chosen Isaiah and equipped him and waits to hear if he will agree. And suddenly, it is easy to agree.

This is the curious forgetting of self that has to happen if we are to walk boldly into the destiny God has prepared for each of us. We must know ourselves, tell the truth about ourselves, love ourselves, we must do all these things—and then we must set ourselves gently aside and commit everything to God's love and power.

If we skip the first part, if we think we can serve God without self-knowledge and self-regard, we will be turned away. Such people cannot serve. We are children of God, in the image of God. First we must come to see this in ourselves. But we cannot stop there. The purpose of faith is not to become a self-satisfied little puddle of self-love. It is, rather, to become a river, a fast-moving, powerful stream of love that flows outward toward the whole world.

THURSDAY IN ADVENT II

Pss 37:1–18 * 37:19–42
Isaiah 7:1–9
2 Thessalonians 2:1–12
Luke 22:1–13

*Do you not remember that I told you
these things when I was still with you?*
2 THESSALONIANS 2:5

My children and grandchildren are patient with my poor memory. They laugh at it, actually, and factor it into their interactions with me. They call me to make sure I've done something I said I would do. They make allowances for my forgetting. They talk me out of my spasms of self-criticism when I forget to do something important.

So does Q. He and I are peers in this aspect of life, capable of forgetting things we have made an elaborate effort to remember. This happens all the time. When it happens, we are tender with each other. Fellow sufferers.

The people who invite me to come and speak may be shocked at the depth of my confusion—I don't know, really, because they are too polite to say so. But they all learn what it takes to get me there: They have to remind me when it is, what I said I would do. They have to remind me who they are. Everything. Regrettably, they have to do all these things each time we speak. How embarrassing. But they are kind about it. *Oh, don't beat yourself up about it,* they say. *I'll re-send the original e-mail.*

So I guess I'm the only one enraged by it. How can I be so stupid? I rail at myself about it. But my rage doesn't improve my memory.

People usually don't shape up in response to a scolding. They usually respond better to encouragement. Usually they already know perfectly well what they've done wrong, and they don't need reminders. Usually they feel badly enough about it already.

As good a rule of thumb as this is to apply to the people you love, it is even better to apply it to yourself. Inner harshness seems not to help us improve; instead, it paralyses us. And it doesn't do other people much good, either. As a mentor used to tell me, *If you love your neighbor and hate yourself, God help your neighbor.*

⌄ FRIDAY IN ADVENT II

Pss 31 * 35
Isaiah 7:10–25
2 Thessalonians 2:13–3:5
Luke 22:14–30

"This is my body, which is given for you.
Do this in remembrance of me."
LUKE 22:19

In my youth, the church's attitude toward children's participation in the Eucharist was different from what it is now. Confirmation was the ticket to communion in those days, and confirmation happened when you were twelve. Before that age, you were kept in the parish hall at Sunday school while the adults had communion, which happened on the first Sunday of each month in my church.

The result of this deprivation was that receiving Communion acquired a tremendous mystique for all of us. One summer, work was being done on the church, and so worship moved into the parish hall. This meant that we would actually witness the communion service. I can still hear the cadence of the priest as he administered the bread and wine: "The Body of our Lord Jesus Christ, which was given for thee . . ." over and over, with such a practiced inflection on each word that it was almost chant. He never sounded like that at any other time, as far as I knew. The familiar walls, the floor, the people—everything seemed suffused with a light the room never had during the parish dinners or Sunday school. It was as if we had been transported to heaven.

The ancient church believed that this was exactly what happened: The Eucharist took the living into the presence of God, where they feasted with the saints. Everyday objects—bread, wine, the table—were transformed and, with the people, became part of something not of this world.

I felt this happen in that little country church. The priest, a low church man if ever there was one, would have disavowed any such thing, I imagine—or would he? It was his dignity and reverence that made me see heaven in the body and blood of Christ and made me long to receive it.

SATURDAY IN ADVENT II

Pss 30:32 * 42, 43
Isaiah 8:1–15
2 Thessalonians 3:6–18
Luke 22:31–38

Do not call conspiracy all that this people calls conspiracy...
ISAIAH 8:12

It never takes long, after something terrible has happened, for the conspiracy theories to sprout like weeds. Some things are simply too resounding in our lives to have just happened, and we find ourselves unable to believe that they were not elaborately planned. Can we really be that vulnerable to chance? Can something upon which we leaned so heavily really be destroyed *by accident?* For no reason? It cannot be. Somebody must have done this. It must have been planned. Paradoxically, we'd rather believe in active evil than in mindless chance. Our plots give us something to oppose and avoid.

So what now? Now that we have been so brutally reminded that some terrible things really *were* carefully planned, that there really *are* people in the world planning our terrible end. Does what used to seem like paranoia now make terrible sense? We know what happened to us physically, but what have the bombings of 9/11 done to us that we can't see?

The answer is in our hands, just as it was before the bombings. We choose the degree of our pessimism and suspiciousness. We decide what is sensible and what is excessive, how to protect ourselves from a world that really is more dangerous than we thought it was. We remove our shoes in the airport, surrender our nail clippers. We do not agree about all of these precautions: Some of them seem excessive, and some of us lose patience with them, making a scene at airport security, even getting ourselves arrested.

And here is this ancient prophet, warning us against leaping to conclusions, against the me-too imputing of guilt to people who have done nothing wrong, simply on the basis of where they are from. Nothing we have endured excuses us from using our common sense and remembering our tradition of fairness when we consider our diverse society, our welcome of the stranger.

SUNDAY, ADVENT III

Pss 63:1–8 (9–11), 98 * 103
Isaiah 13:6–13
Hebrews 12:18–29
John 3:22–30

I will make mortals more rare than fine gold,
and humans than the gold of Ophir.
ISAIAH 13:12

The worldwide sperm count may be going down, the BBC says. Why this is, or if it is even really the case, in uncertain: Maybe the men sampled weren't typical. But why? Is it because of pollution? Food additives? Because of the increase in the number of men in sedentary occupations? Or the increased use of heavy, vibrating machines?

Raised on laments about the dangers of world overpopulation, it is hard to know how to receive this news. Are we on our way out?

Might it be that we've made such a mess of things that we're being ushered off the planet, in favor of another species that might do better? Cats? No, I think not. Dogs? Chimpanzees? Maybe dolphins.

The world could get along beautifully without human beings in it, I think. We have defaced it more than we have helped it: riddled it with holes, cut down its green canopy of trees, fouled its air with our coal furnaces and our SUVs, its water with our chemical wastes.

Although we know it will happen, we cannot imagine the world without us. We cannot even encompass our own individual ends with our imaginations, never mind that of the human race: plants growing in among the abandoned cars, animals nesting in our apartments, our ships floating, directionless, on the face of the sea. Not a human soul in sight.

It will happen. We will become extinct, eventually. Gradually, perhaps, one hopes. But it is more likely to be rather sudden. And at our own hand.

MONDAY IN ADVENT III

Pss 41, 52 * 44
Isaiah 8:16–9:1
2 Peter 1:1–11
Luke 22:39–53

Therefore, brothers and sisters, be all the more eager to confirm your call and election, for if you do this, you will never stumble. For in this way, entry into the eternal kingdom of our Lord and Savior Jesus Christ will be richly provided for you.

2 PETER 1:10–11

"Mary's Command to Catholics" reads the front of the little pamphlet left on the train seat. I pick it up to see what it is that Mary wants us to do. It turns out that the pamphlet is an Evangelical Protestant tract against Roman Catholic practices concerning Mary, the saints, the role of tradition—what Catholics need to do, it says, is believe in Jesus and be saved.

But what does it mean to be saved? Saved from what? Hell, usually, is what threatens us, although it is hard for me to believe that God operates in so simplistic and punitive a manner that an eternal sizzle in Hades is the default fate of human beings, more likely to happen than not to. Or that it is possible to isolate—with such confidence—a tendency among Roman Catholics toward activities that will land them there.

I don't think faith is all about going to heaven or going to hell. I think it is about the love of God wherever we are. About learning to listen and look for the signs of God everywhere. About seeing and serving Christ in our neighbors, near and far. Faith is about giving our lives to God, in all their ambiguity, without being certain of very much at all.

From all the obstacles I throw up to that grace in my life, I need saving. From the crippling effects of my own ego. From my petty warfares. From my selfishness.

Are you saved? Jesus is saving me every day.

TUESDAY IN ADVENT III

Pss 45 * 47, 48
Isaiah 9:1–7
2 Peter 1:12–21
Luke 22:54–69

When they had kindled a fire in the middle of the courtyard and sat down together, Peter sat among them.
LUKE 22:55

I *guess the wood hasn't seasoned long enough,* I mutter as I twist another sheet of newspaper and put it under the logs. A few twigs on top, and I light the match. The paper goes up like a torch, and so does the kindling. Good. But ten minutes later I come back into the room to a sullen smolder.

The older, better wood is all the way at the bottom of the wood-pile. I should have thought ahead last summer, when we were piling the wood. I consider putting a few of the smaller logs into the oven to roast for awhile, but that is simply too counterintuitive a waste of fossil fuel to pursue.

And Q says we lose more heat up the chimney from having a fire than from not having one. How can that be?

Light all the matches you want. Twist the entire Sunday *Times*, piece by piece, into long coils of newsprint and burn them all: If your log isn't ready, it won't burn.

Things don't happen until it's time for them to happen. The Bible has a poetic way of putting it: Things happen *in the fullness of time*. Time ripens history. The unlikely becomes eminently possible. God acts in the ripening of time.

Pleroma is the Greek word for that fullness. Ancient Christians used the term to talk about the consummation of the world—its end, when everything that was becoming has become, when Christ will be all in all. But what if each small ripening in life is part of the *pleroma*? What if the fullness of time is *becoming* every day, little by little, as we live our lives? What if we get to decide every day, or even several times a day, to be a part of its becoming?

Peter thought he had a lock on his relationship with Jesus. But he warmed his hands over a fire with some people he didn't know, and within minutes he had turned his back on the whole thing. Things can't happen in life until their time, and they sometimes won't happen unless we cooperate.

WEDNESDAY IN ADVENT III

Pss 119:49–72 * 49, (53)
Isaiah 9:8–17
2 Peter 2:1–10a
Mark 1:1–8

"Prepare the way of the Lord, make his paths straight ..."
MARK 1:3

It is only four o'clock in the afternoon, but the sunlight is beginning to slant toward evening. Depressing for some people, I know, but I love the early darkness of Advent, love the wildness outside and the golden light inside. I never remember childhood more vividly than I remember it at this time of year: the steady escalation of Christmas preparations at school, the intent crafting of presents, rehearsals of Christmas pageants, the magic of store windows, back when they didn't put Christmas things out in September. The baking, the sending of cards.

Many things are different now, of course. One of the presents my father got for our neighbor was a carton of his favorite cigarettes. Both men are dead now, of diseases related to smoking—I doubt if anyone wraps up a carton of smokes and gives them to anybody today.

The Christmas pageant at the public school was a nativity scene. We sang religious Christmas carols there. Our principal was Jewish. It never occurred to me to wonder if this was difficult for him. There was a nativity scene in the little town, too, and a ceremonial lighting of it each year. Nobody thought it strange.

Christians gripe about how secular our society has become. I just think it's become more fair: It wasn't right to expect non-Christians to participate in our feasts, or to make them feel left out if they didn't. The secular world shouldn't have to educate our children about our faith on our behalf. We should do that ourselves. It should take some effort. And it won't happen for us now, if we don't make the effort. There are children who don't know whose birthday Christmas is, and parents who have never told them.

It was a nice way to grow up—very secure. Unanimous. But the unanimity was fraudulent—we thought everybody was like us, but we could think so only because we were the majority and could ignore the others.

This is better. Among other reasons, it is more like the world into which Jesus came, a world that was no more unanimous in welcoming him than ours is, a world that was decidedly not united in worshipping him. An indifferent world, like ours. And into it he came, anyway. And some believed and taught it to their children. So we could know.

THURSDAY IN ADVENT III

Pss 50 * (59, 60) or 33
Isaiah 9:18–10:4
2 Peter 2:10b–16
Matthew 3:1–12

What will you do on the day of punishment, in the calamity that will come from far away? To whom will you flee for help?

ISAIAH 10:3

The *New York Post* went wild with the capture of Saddam Hussein: "DEATH TO SADDAM," ran one headline. There were front page pictures of the squalid hideout where Hussein spent his last days at large, of two grinning GIs lifting the cover off the hole in which he hid, of the same two looking grimly down into the hole, rifles at the ready: a Saddam's-eye view.

The abrupt toppling of a powerful leader is disconcerting. You mean he's a man, like other men? No cavalry to the rescue, no blindly loyal Republican Guards waiting in the bushes to defend him to the last drop of their own blood? Apparently not.

The grind of war continues. We personalize our enemy: We fight Saddam, Osama, Hitler, as if they were themselves arrayed in the battlefield. *Greetings from President Bush,* one young soldier said as the Iraqi leader looked numbly up at him. But President Bush wasn't there. Just two twenty-year-olds with rifles.

That is what jars us: He has lost the power we feared. He is no match for two young men. He surrenders without a struggle, doesn't fire the pistol he holds in his hand. Is this where worldly power ends up? Can it disappear so quickly? And if it can desert one who held the lives of millions in his grip, what about my puny power? It is a puff of smoke. Any breeze can dissipate it.

We absolutize things that aren't absolute. We think all this will go on forever, and it's all temporary. Forever is something nobody on earth has. Forever belongs to God.

FRIDAY IN ADVENT III

Pss 40, 54 * 51
Isaiah 10:5–19
2 Peter 2:17–22
Matthew 11:2–15

"Go and tell John what you hear and see:
the blind receive their sight, the lame walk . . .
and the poor have good news brought to them."
MATTHEW 11:4–5

The train is full of children returning from "A Christmas Carol" at Madison Square Garden. Many of them sport tiny plastic top hats: The train is awash in little Cratchitts.

Dickens' parable of individual responsibility and societal sin was probably lost on most of them: There is a lot of singing and dancing in this "Christmas Carol." Even the adults who have loved Scrooge and Tiny Tim for decades tend to see it as a story about the softening of one old man's heart. Dickens was dogged by Scrooge throughout his famous life: His audiences never wanted to hear anything else.

But there is much more in this story. It is a serious protest against horrors about which Dickens was all too well-informed: backbreaking child labor, the casual cruelties of class, the lack of protection for the worker.

It was just at the time of *A Christmas Carol* that English society was beginning to consider a new sense of social interdependence. Blood had been shed on behalf of the poor, and those in power realized that reform might be the only alternative to revolution. Dickens himself had been a child worker. He worked in an ink factory and lived apart from his family from a young age, in physical deprivation and terrible loneliness. His Christmas tale, as well as his other writings, ensured that henceforth there would be a moral dimension to poverty, with regard not only to the sufferer himself, but to all who permit or even profit by his anguish.

SATURDAY IN ADVENT III

Pss 55 * 138, 139:1–17 (18–23)
Isaiah 10:20–27
Jude 17–25
Luke 3:1–9

In the fifteenth year of the reign of Emperor Tiberius, when Pontius Pilate was governor of Judea, and Herod was ruler of Galilee, and his brother Philip ruler of the region of Ituraea and Trachonitis, and Lysanias ruler of Abilene, during the high priesthood of Annas and Caiaphas, the word of God came to John son of Zechariah in the wilderness.

LUKE 3:1–2

I have always wondered if this list of celebrities is not intended specifically to contrast with the rustic figure of John the Baptist. All these fancy people, and to whom does the word of God come? And where? Palace? Temple? Synagogue? No, just to weird John out in the wilderness.

This is not our first clue that the coming messiah will be somewhat other than expected. None of the trappings of power as the world understands power are present in any of these old stories. The only royalty present are three vague kings, who may not even have been kings at all, and mad Herod, a one-man commercial for the end of monarchies everywhere.

It is good news for us. The word of God came to John and it can come to me and you. Many things in this world are a matter of who you are and who you know, but not this one. There's not a soul to whom God does not speak. Nobody is without God's guiding word. Discerning it is something else, of course. Almost all of us would follow with alacrity if we knew for sure it was God doing the asking. We never do know for sure, though. We peer into our present and into our past, hoping we will glimpse the direction of our future. We look, but we don't see much.

But maybe we should remember these clues. Remember that he comes where and when he is not expected. To people who are not household words. In simple situations. We may be more important in God's plan than we think we are—John certainly was. Mary was. Joseph was. Maybe me and maybe you.

SUNDAY, ADVENT IV

Pss 24, 29 * 8, 84
Isaiah 42:1–12
Ephesians 6:10–20
John 3:16–21

Put on the whole armor of God, so that you may
be able to stand against the wiles of the devil.
EPHESIANS 6:11

The Occupational Safety and Health Administration (OSHA) center was over in the northwest corner of the site, in what amounted to the middle of West Street. You needed to pay a call there, before you did anything else, to get your respirator. Wearing our respirators, we all looked like Martians: They had two round filters on either side of the nose, and a double strap of rubber that went around your head. When you spoke, it was hard for people to understand you.

So a lot of people didn't wear their respirators. I didn't, mostly—what's the good of a chaplain who can't speak? I figured it was okay not to—I saw lots of firefighters who weren't wearing theirs, either. Once in a while an OSHA person would happen by and scold about it, and then you'd put yours on. Once I dropped mine and a forklift ran over it. I never bothered to go and get another one.

It was dumb to be so casual about protection. There was bad stuff in the air: Some of it you could see and some of it you couldn't. But you could feel it, after a while: a dry sandpapery feeling in your chest. When there is danger, you need protection. It's not brave to forego it. It's stupid.

I think there was something working in us besides garden-variety foolishness, though. A peculiar mortification of the flesh was in the air at Ground Zero, too, an irrational desire to join those who had perished in their suffering. As if our discomfort were a fit offering for them, somehow joining us to them. Reaching them, when nothing else could reach them any more.

I just don't want to hurt him any more, a firefighter told a reporter when asked about the delicacy of extricating the body of a dead colleague from the wreckage. Of course, he cannot be hurt anymore. He is beyond hurting. That is over now, over forever.

And yet. And yet. It was if they were frozen in their last moments. As if we could only meet them there.

I told you it was irrational.

MONDAY IN ADVENT IV

Pss 61, 62 * 112, 115
Isaiah 11:1–9
Revelation 20:1–10
John 5:30–47

A shoot shall come out from the stump of Jesse . . .
ISAIAH 11:1

The trumpet vine in the back garden blew to the ground in a windstorm, snapping its thick trunk like a twig and bending an iron support double with the force of its fall. There was nothing for it but to chop away everything else. Now it looks very odd out there. Trumpet was big, forming an arch under which you could walk easily. And now there's nothing there.

I know that plant, though. He'll be as huge as he ever was come midsummer. The body blow will inspire him to greater fecundity. Out of his devastation will come a better plant.

I never really noticed this verse until I came to know Trumpet. A shoot will come from the stump of Jesse: Life and growth are going to arise straight from the exact place of destruction. Israel was an occupied country, weak and discouraged. It was out of that discouragement that life would come.

Out of your discouragement, too. Out of your devastation. There is life after even the worst thing—not life as it was before, but life that can still have meaning and joy.

At first, it seems disloyal to your former joy even to think of life having meaning again. At first, the urge to immolate ourselves on the pyre of our dead happiness is irresistible. And yes, some time must be spent in marking the injury. But out of the jagged stump of your loss, green shoots of life can grow. Will grow, if you will let them. They do not cancel out former love or old faithfulness. They are cause for rejoicing.

They are signs of God.

TUESDAY IN ADVENT IV

Pss 66, 67 * 116, 117
Isaiah 11:10–16
Revelation 20:11–21:8
Luke 1:5–25

And the sea gave up the dead that were in it . . .
REVELATION 20:13

More than a decade of maritime ministry gave me a permanent love of the sea and those who sail upon it. My eyes automatically scan every waterfront I pass in every city I visit for ships: They stand against the horizon, large as buildings, mistaken for buildings by those unaccustomed to them. I can usually tell who in a crowd has been a seafarer, by the way he stands: legs slightly apart to brace against the roll of the ship. They stand that way even when they're on land. They stand that way years after they've stopped going to sea.

They never know for sure that they will make their next port. If some of them act a little crazy when they come ashore, that's why. But most of them don't come ashore for very long, not any more. A day if they're lucky. They'll head out in the morning. And it is possible that they will not see land again. Seafaring is safer today than it ever has been, but a ship still goes down somewhere in the world every three days.

I have seen old men's eyes fill with tears when they spoke of what they saw on the Murmansk Run during the Second World War—men in the icy water, where nobody could survive for longer than a few minutes. I have been awakened at night by a call from the Coast Guard about a ship that went down with all hands in twenty-foot seas.

Many, many sailors sleep forever in the sea: thousands, from every age that has ever sailed. Those who loved them had no grave at which to weep. Just the vastness of the water.

But in this strange vision of the end of time, a word of comfort: The sea will give up her dead. Those who left so suddenly from life—they will not be left out at the end.

WEDNESDAY IN ADVENT IV

Pss 72 * 111, 113
Isaiah 28:9–22
Revelation 21:9–21
Luke 1:26–38

"Greetings, favored one! The Lord is with you."
LUKE 1:28

This is how a "Hail Mary" goes: *Hail, Mary, full of grace, the Lord is with thee! Blessed art thou among women, and blessed is the fruit of thy womb, Jesus. Holy Mary, mother of God, pray for us sinners now and at the hour of our death.*

Somewhere in the south of France, I forget where now, I was in the church, examining the frescoes. After a time, I slipped into one of the chairs and sat, soaking up the feel of the place.

Women began to arrive—ten or twelve of them, one or two at a time. Not young women: The youngest was fifty and the eldest was old. They sat in the first two or three rows of seats in front of Mary's statue in the side chapel.

When all appeared to be present, they began. I had not noticed that each woman carried a rosary in her hand. Each one sat erect in her chair, eyes upon the Virgin Mother, hands busy in her lap.

One woman began and the others took it up after the first line. Their voices were younger than they were, chanting the words in the singsong of schoolgirls reciting a poem: a girlish, dutiful cadence learned years ago and carried intact past marriage, motherhood, old age. Always just as it was. There was no need to change it, to try to make it sound more adult or more meaningful. Its meaning was in their saying it together throughout a lifetime. It needed no more meaning than that.

I came closer and sat behind the last row of women. I began to recite the rosary along with them. Over and over we said it, on and on. Each woman by turn had the recitation, with the others falling in at the proper time. When the woman a few seats before me took her turn, I arose quietly and left, embarrassed by my French. Didn't want to get it wrong. They continued their recitation.

I wish I had stayed.

THURSDAY IN ADVENT IV

Pss 80 * 146, 147
Isaiah 29:13–24
Revelation 21:22–22:5
Luke 1:39–48a (48b–56)

My soul magnifies the Lord.
LUKE 1:46

Getting everything done on time and perfectly is not as important as it feels. We experience December 25 as a drop-dead deadline, the date by which everything must be finished.

But it's not. It's really the date when things begin. And perfection has little to do with love and enjoyment of each other. All opinion to the contrary is really marketing, attempts to sell us on the idea that the primary gifts of the season are the ones we buy. They are not. The primary Christmas gift is the first one we received: the love that came down at Christmas to embrace the whole world. All the rest is in response to that first gift.

Get this right and you will not be frazzled and distracted by Christmas preparations. Keep your eyes on the prize, and the rest will fall into place as needed.

And when your friends ask you if you've done everything? When they present you with something perfect? When it's obvious that they spent more money on you than you spent on them, and that old anxiety knocks at your door, whispering that you didn't do Christmas right, didn't do it perfectly? Hints that the giving of gifts is really a commercial transaction, a tit-for-tat business deal?

Tell it to leave you alone. Tell it that it's Christmas. Lock it in the closet if it won't be quiet. And tell your friend thank you, and compliment her on her lovely taste. And then tell her exactly what it is that you love most about her.

FRIDAY IN ADVENT IV

Pss 93, 96 * 148, 150
Isaiah 33:17–22
Revelation 22:6–11, 18–20
Luke 1:57–66

I fell down to worship at the feet of the angel . . .
but he said to me, "You must not do that!
I am a fellow servant with you . . . Worship God!"
REVELATION 22:8, 9

Angels are easier to take than God, we think: pretty blonde people with wings. Many people with no other formal belief system at all have a colorful and quite detailed belief in angels and their doings.

Especially the guardian angel. Everybody has one, some think, and the guardian angel gets you out of the trouble you get yourself into. I don't know what happens, under this system of belief, when we die—maybe the angel went off duty. Because the idea of a guardian angel, although an appealing one, is not a feature of Christian teaching. Guardian angels are fairytale creatures, not scriptural ones.

Angels are instinctively and supremely obedient to God. Completely uninterested in themselves—this is how we know they are not our deceased relatives, another common fantasy: None of our relatives were that selfless. Angels are created that way. They weren't formerly anything but what they are now.

Are they real? I have no idea. I suppose it depends in part on what you think "real" is. Certainly they have been in our thoughts and stories for a long, long time. They have been a foil to the impulsiveness and self-aggrandizement that we cannot help but see when we examine ourselves. Angels are what we would be if we did not have those faults.

But of course, they are not earthly, the angels. They are not tempted as we are. Created to be what they are, they are not plunged into our compromises and ambiguities. They have no option but the good.

So we are not angels, but neither was Jesus. Tempted in every way as we are, it says in the Book of Common Prayer: really tempted, just as we are really tempted. The life into which Christ came was hard for him, as ours is hard. Harder than theirs, we think—of course, we don't walk in their shoes. Fly with their wings—whatever. We're not them. And we're not him. We are in between the Son of God and the choiceless angels of God. The children of God is what we are.

CHRISTMAS EVE

Pss 45, 46* 89:1–29
Isaiah 35:1–10 * Isaiah 59:15b–21
Revelation 22:12–17, 21* Philippians 2:5–11
Luke 1:67–80

"See, I am coming soon. . . ."
REVELATION 22:12

All I have to do is put up the evergreen garlands on the porch, assemble a year's worth of reimbursement vouchers, shop for Christmas dinner, hear a handful of confessions, write seven sermons and deliver two of them, and maybe make another batch of pralines and some gingerbread men. Oh, and finish this book, which is about 150 pages short and due in seven days. Oh, my.

I resolved sometime in July to keep December as clear as possible, so I could have a life closer to home and finish this book. And I have kept closer to home. It's the book and the life I haven't yet mastered.

What were the ancient rhythms of the day? They worked hard, we know, just to maintain the necessities of life. No food you didn't make yourself, no cloth you didn't weave. Such limitations kept things simple.

And yet, they didn't stay simple. Nothing ever does. Soon bakers did the bread for everyone, and tailors made the clothing. Shoemakers, millers: Work became more and more specialized. Complexity: It's just what human beings do.

Maybe they were onto something. I look again at the to-do list in the first paragraph of this little essay: One reason for its length is that I plan to bake instead of buy, to hold onto tasks I could farm out. But it is those tasks I most want to do. Those tasks are part of having a life.

I know: You do my reimbursement vouchers. I'll bake the cookies. At this late date, neither of us is going to finish everything we told ourselves we'd do. Never mind. On Christmas Eve, you can only afford to do the ones close to your heart. The others will have to fend for themselves.

Christmas

CHRISTMAS DAY

Pss 2, 85 * 110:1–5 (6–7), 132
Zechariah 2:10–13
1 John 4:7–16
John 3:31–36

In this is love, not that we loved God but that he loved us. . . .
1 JOHN 4:10

Lots of people don't know that God loves them. They don't ordinarily give it much thought: It seems childish to think of such a thing, superstitious, even selfish. Who am I to imagine that God loves me? It seems safer to think of God in much more impersonal terms—a force, a life spirit that permeates everything. Energy, like electricity or nuclear power. Something a lot more scientific than love.

But behind this becoming modesty is fear. The only loves we know about come and go, stay just long enough for us to get connected to them and then—*poof!*—gone. To us, love is undependable.

But God's love isn't like ours. God isn't buffeted by change, as we are. We may be blown around by every wind that comes along, but God stays still. There is nothing behind God, nowhere for God to hide from us, and no reason for God to hide.

Sometimes it helps us to grasp the possibility of God's love if we choose to proceed for a time as if it were true. To take the love of God as a working hypothesis in life and see what happens. And what happens is this: More and more things begin to look like love. The good and the beautiful begin to seem intentional. There is no proof of this, no evidence not previously available. You don't know a single thing you didn't know before. You just arrange what you know differently, order it under a different assumption.

You can always go back, you know. You don't have to think about the love of God if you don't want to. Nobody's going to make you.

But you can also stay. You can stay forever.

DECEMBER 26, FEAST OF ST. STEPHEN

Pss 28, 30 * 118
2 Chronicles 24:17–22 * Wisdom 4:7–15
Acts 6:1–7 * Acts 7:59–8:8

The righteous, though they die early, will be at rest.
For old age is not honored for length of time, or measured
by number of years; but understanding is gray hair
for anyone, and a blameless life is ripe old age.
WISDOM 4:7–9

So that's it—those who die young aren't really young. Their lives are complete, even though they are cut short in time.

Ridiculous and infuriating, such talk—unless you've spent a long, long time thinking about a particular young life that ended too soon. Then, sometimes, when your mood is right, such a thing begins to make a certain odd sense: He didn't live long enough to suit me, by any means. Not near long enough. By rights, I was supposed to die first. Absolutely.

But his life was complete in itself. For his age, he was complete. People aren't complete just because they live to be a ripe old age. They're complete in the moment they have. She never got to be twenty-four. But she was a beautiful twenty-three. He was the complete three-year-old. He was the complete teenager. She was herself—I would have added nothing to her except more time with her. I wouldn't have changed a thing.

The bereaved have abundant leisure time to ponder such things. We make absurd bargains with God about things that are past, as if we could work out a deal and change what has happened. What if it had been me driving, instead? What if I had gotten that virus, instead? What if she'd gone to that other college—she'd still be alive. And we pretend she *did* go to the other school, the one that didn't have a fire in the dormitory, that we really *were* the one driving, that a freak virus didn't savage her. We pretend he went on to graduate, that the wedding did take place, that she made it to fourth grade. Became a lawyer championing the rights of those disabled with his own disability, and kicked butt, let me tell you. Pretend for a while, and imagine. It doesn't change anything. None of these wonderful things happened. But it relieves the ache, sometimes, and we think relieving the ache is important.

Stephen was young. Too young to die, certainly: just starting out in his new life as a deacon. Good and passionate about his calling. Full of everything fine. What wouldn't he have been had he lived! His parents must have had these very thoughts. But he didn't live. He died. Complete, at a very young age.

And it is his completeness we remember, even now.

DECEMBER 27,
FEAST OF ST JOHN

Pss 97, 98 * 145
Proverbs 8:22–30 * Isaiah 44:1–8
John 13:20–35 * 1 John 5:1–12

*This one will say, "I am the Lord's"; another will be called
by the name of Jacob; yet another will write on the hand,
"The Lord's," and adopt the name Israel.*

ISAIAH 44:5

It is 8:00 in the morning in New York and 1 P.M. in London. This is the second day of the two-day summit of Anglican Primates to deal with the action of the American House of Bishops in approving Gene Robinson's election as Bishop of New Hampshire. Perhaps there will be some news in mid-afternoon, New York time.

I have had several e-mails from outside the communion asking about the designation "primates." Some have mentioned lemurs, chimpanzees, and other intelligent animals of the same phylum. Others have asked if such a title isn't a tad too hierarchical for our century. I don't imagine the second concern troubles many of the Primates. They have never expressed an opinion on the first. My advice is to let it go: The Church is an outfit that calls a lobby a "narthex," a goblet a "chalice," a plate a "paten" and a breadbox a "ciborium." Its priests wear ponchos, which they call "chasubles," made of fabrics otherwise used only in curtains. You're not going to change them.

They may, however, change themselves. Or they may not. Something, though, will come out of the meeting in London, and Anglicans all over the world are watching and waiting. And arguing. Threatening to leave and threatening to stay. Calling each other names.

The time for argument is over. I do believe just about everything that could be said on either side of the argument about homosexuality in the church has been said, hundreds of times in hundreds of places. We have done that.

I believe that prayer is now the only thing left to people who are worried about the outcome of this meeting—and worried, in general, about what is ahead. Prayer is the only thing left, and it is fortunate that prayer is a mighty thing. Its might, though, is manifest to us in strange and indirect ways. God's response to prayer is not immediate and clear, as we wish it were. The reason for this lies not in God's inability to express himself, but in our inability to understand. This is not our fault. God is God. We are only primates.

In praying about this or any other controversy in your life, consider praying first for the one with whom you disagree. Think about praying first for the one who infuriates you. And pray for that person or group of people without an agenda of your own—don't pray that they might see the error of their ways and repent, or that God might give them all a walloping case of intestinal flu. Don't pray anything specific for them. You don't need to. The madder you are about it, the more assiduously you should avoid any words at all in your prayer for your enemy. Leave the details to God. God doesn't need our suggestions anyway—he is fully informed about our affairs. We don't need to tell God things. God knows.

Just name them before God. Picture them, if you can. Picture them in the hands of God—literally—if you have that kind of childish ability to imagine. Just lift them up to God for blessing, the same blessing for which you yourself long. You need do nothing beyond this in prayer.

Something interesting will happen if you do this: Your foe will become a human being to you. He will cease to be a cartoon of his offense. You will come to understand that there is more to him than the part you despise. This is the beginning of healing. And there is more: Something happens in your foe when you pray as well. Not something you can predict or control, but there is an ecology of prayer: Change something, and everything changes, just a little. A lot, sometimes. You have to be foolish enough and brave enough to take the counterintuitive step of praying with humility and without words for someone you can't stand. For those who can summon such foolishness and such courage, a miracle awaits.

Spend some time in the prayer for your enemy, in these days of high emotion and hot temper. Have the courage to present your adversary to God and trust that God knows our hearts—all of our hearts—and that Christ is, as we have always maintained, the Lord of history. Nothing can happen, in the church or in the world, that is beyond the mercy of God to heal. Nothing is beyond the power of God to turn what happens in human affairs to possibility and good.

The healing and goodness of God is hard for us to grasp sometimes. Sometimes it's so obvious to us what should happen, and we are heartbroken and angry when something else happens instead. But God is never absent from anything that happens. God is around here someplace. Dry your eyes and look around. Listen. There is an unexpected good here.

DECEMBER 28,
FEAST OF THE HOLY INNOCENTS

Pss 2, 26 * 19, 126
Isaiah 49:13–23 * Isaiah 54:1–13
Matthew 18:1–14 * Mark 10:13–16

So it is not the will of your Father in heaven
that one of these little ones should be lost.
MATTHEW 18:14

I keep finding Christmas gifts I forgot to give people. I drop off two cool tee shirts and a pair of yellow gloves over at my daughter's house for the grandchildren, unwrapped. I don't know what to do with the scented vacuum cleaner beads (you put them in your vacuum cleaner bag and it smells good) or the matching dryer sheets, both in a fragrance called "Beach House." Seems silly to mail them now.

It seems silly, too, to bake Christmas cookies after Christmas. But we've eaten almost all of them, and I've grown accustomed to having them around. I will be strong, though. If there's something I need less than Christmas cookies, I don't know what it is.

I guess I really don't want it to be over. More than old enough to know better, and more than tired enough, I still love it all. Although some of the saddest things in my life have happened at this time of year, it doesn't matter. If anything, the memory of those sorrows makes what is lovely even lovelier.

After all, this story was first written about people who were having a hard time. An unplanned pregnancy. A bitter political situation. Poverty and homelessness. Life was hard then, too, and it would have been easy to give up. Bitter and easy.

But nobody did. Mary and Joseph toughed it out. The shepherds didn't just grunt and turn over to try and get some sleep after the angelic interruption; they jumped up and went to see for themselves, full of hope.

What in their impoverished lives, do you suppose, made them all so hopeful? Today's feast commemorates just how cruel life can be to people who haven't done a thing to deserve it. Not a thing. But still we have hope.

However cruel the world is, the little Savior was saved today. The story can continue.

CHRISTMAS I

Pss 93, 96 * 34
Isaiah 62:6–7, 10–12
Hebrews 2:10–18
Matthew 1:18–25

Her husband Joseph, being a righteous man and unwilling to expose her to public disgrace, planned to dismiss her quietly.
MATTHEW 1:19

Long-suffering Joseph represents bewildered conventionality, up against something way over its head. All he wanted to do was get married. Simple. People had been getting married for centuries. So why was nothing about this engagement going according to plan? Every couple has little setbacks, but why, he must have wondered, couldn't just one thing happen the way it was supposed to? Just one?

The most remarkable thing about Joseph is how able he is to learn. He is permeable. When he tries something and it fails, he is willing to take instruction from a dream. He doesn't insist that the collapse of his own plans is the last word: He is willing to stand corrected.

And to question authority. His instructions about what to do with his young bride, caught in what looked to everyone like fairly convincing evidence of adultery, were clear: Get rid of her. No one would have blamed him in the least.

It should be harder for Christians to submit meekly than it is. All through the stories of the birth of Christ, we find people breaking the rules. Nine out of ten Christians, though, still think that following the rules is what it's all about. If Joseph had assumed that and been unable to go beyond them, what would have happened? To be sure, he would have been blameless, but it makes you wonder: Is our life supposed to be a blameless life? The certainty of a blameless life comes only with never taking a risk. Is that what we're supposed to do?

I doubt it. I think we're supposed to try to do good, and I think we're going to get it wrong, probably many times. I think God is neither surprised nor repelled by our failures, but stays with us and continues to guide us, right up to the end.

DECEMBER 29

Pss 18:1–20 * 18:21–50
Isaiah 12:1–6
Revelation 1:1–8
John 7:37–52

*Surely God is my salvation; I will trust,
and will not be afraid, for the Lord God is my strength
and my might; he has become my salvation.*

ISAIAH 12:2

I buy some vitamin C serum and some wrinkle reducing cream with something called Retinol in it. The vitamin C is supposed to make my skin glow, and we'll just see what the wrinkle reducer will do. But wait—they're both supposed to go on at night, after I wash my face. Oh, no—which one is supposed to go on first? Do I reduce wrinkles on a face that's already glowing? Or do I add a sunny glow to a wrinkle-free one? Will I lose the magic if I apply these cosmetic miracles in the wrong order?

But perhaps I am overestimating the degree of magic I should expect. I am an easy mark for purveyors of cosmetic products, yet another example of the triumph of hope over experience.

My granddaughters have skin as smooth as milk. Not a wrinkle. *Why do you ever wear makeup,* I ask for the millionth time. *People wear makeup to get skin that looks like yours does without any.* I remember my own satiny skin as a young person; I, too, caked it with enough goo that it looked as if I had applied it with a putty knife, circled my eyes with black pencil, drew fish tails bigger than Cleopatra's at the outer corners of them.

Mostly girls wear makeup and smear cream on their faces because it's fun. It's a form of painting. They think they look older in it. And then when they are older, they hope they look younger.

Our earnestness about our looks is pathetic. They have nothing to do with anything of lasting importance about us, but we fret about how we look constantly. We give it the worry we might be expected to give . . . salvation. As if that's what it were.

DECEMBER 30

Pss 20, 21:1–7 (8–14) * 23, 27
Isaiah 25:1–9
Revelation 1:9–20
John 7:53–8:11

Then the Lord God will wipe away the tears from all faces . . .
ISAIAH 25:8

"Pray for peace," I write on the flyleaf of my book about the war. Sometimes a book demands its own author's inscription, and this one is like that: You just don't sign a book that opens with the destruction of the World Trade Center with "Best Wishes!" or "xxoo" or even "To Mary, Happy Birthday."

There are still happy birthdays during a war, of course. Surviving parents worked hard to provide them for their bewildered children in the months following the bombing. Firefighters and cops went awkwardly to the parties for their buddies' kids and then home to their own kids, coming into the house, going right upstairs to their children's rooms, standing by their beds and looking at the sleeping faces, wondering what crazed providence had preserved their lives and let their friends die. They wondered that every day. They still wonder, and they will never know.

And now, the next inevitable act: one soldier a day, sometimes more than one, struck down. Other husbands and wives, other numb children who must struggle toward new kinds of happy birthdays, different sorts of merry Christmases than they ever imagined.

But every loss becomes a part of life, sooner or later. People find new ways to live, and they find ways to make meaningful lives. They don't want just to pass the time. They astonish themselves with what they can absorb and how they can keep loving after having lost what they had always said they couldn't live without.

Pray for peace. Pray that this strange war will end. And pray for inner peace for those whose lives have been shattered by it. Peace, it turns out, is a grittier thing than we thought.

DECEMBER 31, EVE OF HOLY NAME

Pss 46, 48 * 90
Isaiah 26:1–9 * Isaiah 65:15b–25
2 Corinthians 5:16–6:2 * Revelation 21:1–6
John 8:12–19

*"To the thirsty I will give water as a gift
from the spring of the water of life."*
REVELATION 21:6

A bottle of water costs $3 in a Broadway theater. A dollar, in one of the little *bodegas* along Ninth Avenue. $1.50 in Penn Station. It's still free out of the tap—*I'll have the Giuliani,* people in restaurants used to quip during the previous mayoral administration. But nobody ever says *I'll have the Bloomberg* now. I guess it only works with an Italian mayor.

We can't live without it. Food, yes—for quite a while. But not water. There's something a little cold-blooded about selling it, an uncomfortable harbinger of what might someday be: water only for those who can afford to buy it. It's happening in some parts of the world, right now, where the pattern of rain and runoff is changing while the cities that depend on them stay put. Almost all the migration of people in Africa is caused by changes in the water supply. They must have it, so they pack up and move: a desperate act.

Our faith was born in the desert. Those people knew what it was to need water desperately. For them to say that life with Christ is like drinking water is no small thing. And that longing for him was like being thirsty—also no small thing in that part of the world.

We know that what they thought they needed was not what they got. Jesus would not be the military champion of their doomed cause. Israel's end as a nation was near—they would not triumph. There would be no miracle at the end and their longing couldn't change that. Instead, they would be dispersed to the four corners of the earth, their temple destroyed, their religion changed forever. It all looked like failure.

But, in the end, it was not permanent failure. No failure is permanent—it all becomes part of the stuff of life, building blocks of the future. God continues to build and create new things, regardless of how things look from here. One of the new things was the tiny band of Jesus' friends and followers who set forth from the Holy Land into the rest of the world. Tiny and unprepossessing as they were, tonight would be just another night, had it not been for them.

ⅴ FEAST OF THE HOLY NAME

Pss 103 * 148
Genesis 17:1–12a, 15–16
Colossians 2:6–12
John 16:23b–30

As you therefore have received Christ Jesus the Lord,
continue to live your lives in him, rooted and
built up in him and established in the faith . . .
COLOSSIANS 2:6–7

Something about this time of year makes us resolve to do all manner of things better. Almost all our good intentions will be history in a week or two. But there is also that other aspect of this time of year, the part that taps us on the shoulder and whispers that our lives are speeding away, faster and faster, evaporating as we speak. That there is not much time left. That soon we will be gone.

At the end of the year we remember the other years. Look at photos of people who are gone. See our young selves—they, too, are gone. We marvel at them. Was that party really sixty years ago? Was I ever that young?

Yes, comes the answer from the pictures. You were. You still are. I'm still here, inside you, your eighteen-year-old self. But remember, we are leaving soon. Good-bye, good-bye.

Kate the cat cries for her breakfast. I look at the clock as Q gets up to feed her—6:30. Not bad. We learned yesterday that there is such a thing as acupuncture for cats. Maybe it would help her crying out, if it's about her arthritis. Kate is seventeen.

And if her wails are about leaving this life? Will acupuncture ease that pain?

Ah. The only remedy for that sorrow is a life well lived now. "Love well that which thou must leave ere long," Shakespeare wrote, and he was right.

Don't let a day of the new year pass without marking it, because it will be gone when it is over. Put into your days the things you want there—no one else will fill them for you. Anything we have can be taken from us at a moment's notice. Some of the people in our old photographs are dead already, and one day we will be, as well, and no one knows when.

But today is ours.

CHRISTMAS II

Pss 66, 67 * 145
Ecclesiasticus 3:3–9, 14–17
1 John 2:12–17
John 6:41–47

And the world and its desire are passing away. . . .
1 JOHN 2:17

I suppose Jesus sometimes spoke plainly. The Sermon on the Mount is plain. But it has been a long time since he spoke, and the world is very different now. We don't always know what he meant.

And of course, he didn't often give people instructions. Mostly he told stories and left them to draw their own conclusions. So not everyone got it, even then.

Do we wish he had been more clear? Is it really his lack of clarity that prevents us from following him? We would like to think so.

But I doubt it. The fact is, what Jesus asks of us is hard. We don't want to love our enemies. We don't think it's wise not to worry about what we are to eat or what we are to wear. We find it hard to trust God radically, as Jesus does. As Jesus wants us to do. We're uncomfortable with the lens under which Jesus examines us, unwilling to look at ourselves through it. You mean being angry is like killing? Lusting in the heart is like adultery? Forget it. I give up.

Mark Twain once said that it was not the things he didn't understand in scripture that kept him from being a Christian, but the things he understood all too well. We want to receive, and Christianity is all about learning to give. Christ calls us to truth, but we find it so easy to lie. We want to win, but we follow one who lost everything the world holds dear. There's no money in that.

JANUARY 2

Pss 34 * 33
Genesis 12:1–7
Hebrews 11:1–12
John 6:35–42, 48–51

"I am the bread of life. Whoever comes
to me will never be hungry . . ."
JOHN 6:35

"Bread of Life" is a relatively new hymn, one that arose out of the charismatic renewal movement in the 1960s. Do you know it?

I am the bread of life
They who come to me shall not hunger,
They who believe in me shall not thirst,
No one can come to me,

Unless the Father bring them.
And I will raise them up,
On the last day.

The hope in it is palpable. Physical. Completely trusting: It is as if
we were children again. I have friends, though, who find themselves
pausing during some of the verses, and some friends who just leave
this one out: "Unless you eat of the flesh of the Son of Man, and
drink of his blood, you shall not have life within you."

Meaning what? That non-Christians have no hope of eternal
life? That the life of Christ is not for everyone, only for those who
are observant in a certain kind of worship?

I suspect that the bread of life and the blood of Christ, present
for us in the consecrated elements of bread and wine, are not to be
understood only in terms of celebrations of the Holy Eucharist.
This passage from the sixth chapter of John's gospel isn't really
about going to church and taking communion. Hundreds of years
before the gospel was written, thousands of years before the song
was written, the nameless writer/editor of Proverbs talked of the
bread and wine of wisdom: "Come, eat of my bread and drink of
the wine I have mixed. Lay aside immaturity, and live, and walk in
the way of insight" (9:5–6).

Take it within you. Drink deeply of the Spirit of God, and fill yourself with the living presence of God, so that God is actually in you, as
bread is in you when you eat it. Fill your life with it. Let your spirit be
so open to God that you find God everywhere, within you and without you. You carry God with you when you leave this place, wherever
you go. Be Christ for those who meet you in the week to come.

JANUARY 3

Pss 68 * 72
Genesis 28:10–22
Hebrews 11:13–22
John 10:7–17

"I am the good shepherd . . . I know my own and my own know me."
JOHN 10:11, 14

Kate, of all people, deigned to climb into my lap and let me cuddle her yesterday morning. And she actually climbed up on the bed and let me stroke her chin last night. Kate is a bony seventeen. I stroke her thin body, her jawline where cats have special glands that they like to rub on things. She stays with me and purrs loudly. I am grateful, as if she had done me some enormous favor.

And perhaps she has. The days grow shorter and the dark comes early. It is a great comfort to be in bed early, the windows black squares in which you see nothing of the outdoors, the lamps inside casting shadows on the wall around their golden circles of light. This is a cuddly time of year.

In the ancient past, we were close to animals. People brought their farm animals into their houses, literally: The stable was often the bottom floor, and the people lived right above it. You could hear the animals and smell them. In the winter, you could feed them downstairs in a warm place, about as warm as your place was, about as warm as any inside place was going to get in the cold of winter.

Kate cries in the morning for her breakfast. And cries at other times, too: loud, guttural cries of unspecific anguish. I think it's her arthritis.

Or maybe Kate is just raging against the dying of the light, struck with sorrow sometimes at the knowledge that she must soon leave this world. Maybe she knows she's old and growing tiny, shrinking out of this life and into the next one. I certainly know it: I stroke her, feel her tiny bones through her beautiful fur, fight against loving her because I don't want to lose her, lose the battle against love. Again. I always lose.

The sun comes up in the morning. By 10:00 it spills through the upstairs window, where many of the geraniums spend the winter. Kate finds a place in between two pots and curls up in it, in a pool of warm sun. She stays there all day, until the sun goes down and it grows dark. Perhaps she will come and cuddle with me again. I hope so. We could keep each other warm.

JANUARY 4

Pss 85, 87 * 89:1–29
Exodus 3:1–12
Hebrews 11:23–31
John 14:6–14

"I am the way, and the truth, and the life.
No one comes to the Father except through me."
JOHN 14:6

I remember it well: I was still in seminary, and the terrible incident was the talk of the refectory. We had been reading admiring first-century accounts of the desperate last stand of the doomed Jews at Masada, when parents killed their babies and then themselves, rather than to fall into the hands of the Romans who had surrounded them. When the conquerors entered the fortress, they found nobody there who was still alive.

Why did modern people drink poison so willingly in Jonestown? Give it to their children, their aged parents? How was it that they couldn't see that their leader was crazy? And we thought of our own tradition, of Masada, of the many instances in which people in scripture kill others rather than let them fall away from God, and we paused, the hair standing up on the backs of our necks.

On the radio last night, a community member who happened to be away from the compound on that terrible last day was interviewed. "What are your thoughts now about what happened in Jonestown?" the interviewer asked her, gently. The woman began to cry. "I'm so sorry for all the people who died," she said. "There's nothing I can do to make it right." But she tried to make the interviewer understand how strong a thing it was to live in a community like that. How much joy there was, especially at first. What it meant to a young black woman to live in a community with no racism, in which love and understanding were preached and lived. It wasn't crazy, she said, not at first. It was wonderful. We were so happy.

I believe I understand how that could be. To know we are beloved of God and one another—nothing is sweeter. I can understand never wanting to lose that. And if I thought that sweetness lived only in one place, I believe I can understand how easy it would be to overlook the signs of other things I didn't want to see. I wouldn't want to see the insanity. I would be too committed to the love and security I needed to see it.

This is what happens when a community walls itself off from the world. This is what happens when "the world" becomes a pejorative term. When we refuse to be informed by everything God sets before us to teach us, when we begin to insist on receiving information only from the sources we choose, that we can decide how God will and will not speak to us—we begin to be insane. The insanity begins even if that source is Holy Scripture, for it is not the Bible that's crazy: It's us. When we put it to uses for which it was not written, it can no longer help us, can no longer teach us its love and faithfulness. We begin to think it teaches us other things.

JANUARY 5,
EVE OF EPIPHANY

Pss 2, 110:1–5 (6–7) * 29, 98
Joshua 1:1–9 * Isaiah 66:18–23
Hebrews 11:32–12:2 * Romans 15:7–13
John 15:1–16

May the God of hope fill you with all joy and peace in believing . . .
ROMANS 15:13

Inexplicably, some hummingbirds don't go south in the winter. Some of them just decide to stay here, once in a while. What makes a hummingbird decide just not to go south, I wonder. "Mexico is just so over," she says to her friends, and they all look at her in disbelief as a chill wind ruffles their tiny feathers: There's a reason why instinctive behavior is instinctive. And, in a few days, they all take off, leaving her behind. She flits around the garden for a few days, pretending she doesn't mind being the only hummingbird for miles around. Then—"Wait for me!"—she takes off.

But sometimes she doesn't. Sometimes they really do stay up here. They do this by going into people's houses and living there all winter. I have a book about a lady who invited one in for the winter and ended up becoming a full-time hummingbird nurse and hostess, cordoning off a whole room in her house for the hummers.

I would do that. I'd give them any room they wanted—they could choose. But there are no hummingbirds at the Geranium Farm. Not in the winter and not even in the summer. Their red feeders are cleaned and packed away now. I have quite a collection of hummingbird feeders at which no hummingbird has ever fed. All summer, I boil water and sugar together and fill them carefully. I attract lots of ants, but no hummingbirds.

It is odd that an enterprise that fails so consistently to bear fruit doesn't discourage me more. But it does not. My heart doesn't sink in discouragement when I hang yet another garish red plastic pie plate with yellow flowers on its metal hook. I never say "Oh, what's the use? They'll never come." Because I don't know that, do I? They might come at this very moment.

What is hope? It sticks its neck out and looks foolish in pursuit of life, not in retreat from it. Oddly, it is not embittered by not succeeding. Somehow, it is enough for me to know that there are hummingbirds in the world, that they are living and drinking from flowers and other people's weird plastic feeders somewhere, even if they are not doing so in my garden. Even if they never do. Just thinking about them and preparing for them makes me happy.

I believe I love them with a godly love. I think that's what God's love must feel like to God: delight in the very existence of the other, whether or not you ever possess it. It is enough that they are in the world.

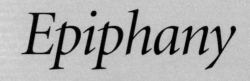

Epiphany

FEAST OF THE EPIPHANY

Pss 46, 97 * 96, 100
Isaiah 52:7–10
Revelation 21:22–27
Matthew 12:14–21

*The Pharisees went out and conspired
against [Jesus], how to destroy him.*
MATTHEW 12:14

Jesus' consistent offense, as far as his countrymen were concerned, was suggesting, in word and deed, that other people besides the chosen people may receive God's saving grace. Bringing healing to people who weren't children of Abraham. Associating with Samaritans. Reminding people of suggestions in the Hebrew scriptures that this might be true: "In his name will the Gentiles hope." Suggesting that his hearers' ancient assumptions about God's promise to Israel might work against them, rendering them unable to see and understand what was really before them. And, as if on cue, they began to plot against his life.

Ours is a gentler age. Our folks usually just withhold their pledges.

There's an old theatre saying: *It's not enough that I succeed; my friends must also fail.* Jesus' great offense was suggesting that God's love was wide enough to include people his hearers might not want to include. We can't stand that. At the very least, God must agree to dislike the people we dislike. He must let us decide who is in and who is out. At our worst, we care more about excluding sinners from salvation than we do about being saved ourselves.

Wisely, God has not left that choice to us. God scandalizes us with the breadth of his love. We want to be the ones who set the rules for its action in the world, but God gently takes that power out of our hands every time we make a grab for it.

Be careful: You are never in more danger than when you think you know what God can and cannot do. Will and will not do. Does and does not love. There are many more things about God that we do not know than things we do. The only reasonable posture for us is complete humility, coupled with alert expectation and clear vision. God is alive, and God is good. Those two things are what make our journey an adventure. We choose some of the fellow travelers on our journey. And God chooses some of the others. And grants us the blessing of all of them along the way.

JANUARY 7

Pss 103 * 114, 115
Isaiah 52:3–6
Revelation 2:1–7
John 2:1–11

When the wine gave out, the mother of Jesus
said to him, "They have no wine."
JOHN 2:3

Sometimes people are a little disappointed in the wedding at Cana: Shouldn't Jesus' first miracle have been about something more serious than catering a wedding reception? It sounds like Jesus may have thought so, too: "Woman, what concern is that to you and to me? My hour has not yet come" (John 2:4).

But ours is an incarnational faith. Jesus came into a world that was full of pain, it is true, but sometimes the world he came into is just annoying, and this was one of those times. He really was human. He went to parties and drank wine. His mom nagged him a little and he snapped at her.

The Church requires a minimum of three hours premarital counseling by the priest who will perform the ceremony. You talk with them about their relationship and their future, their hopes, their values, the way they handle disagreement, and above all, encourage them not to get so sucked into the wedding that the marriage takes a back seat. Get plenty of rest, you say, and be sure you get plenty of time just together, alone, without all the wedding stuff. This is your wedding, you say a dozen times, not your mom's. Do what you think best. Trust each other. Trust yourself. See the forest, as well as the trees.

The wedding won't be perfect. Something will be amiss. Maybe something big, maybe not. Maybe you'll run out of wine. Maybe something else. The wedding will be just like life: beautiful, unique, flawed. It is the flaw about which you will joke in the years to come. If the wedding day is to be joyful, it will be because you have decided to embrace the flaw, to encompass it, not to allow it to stand alone and draw attention to itself for the rest of your life.

This is as good a way as any to begin a new life. There will be other flaws to embrace and encompass, other things that seek to dominate your spirit and distract you from being present to the beauty of each day. The married and the single alike have them, and everybody must learn to embrace and encompass them. Otherwise they will be all you see, and you'll miss the wonder.

JANUARY 8

Pss 117, 118 * 112, 113
Isaiah 59:15–21
Revelation 2:8–17
John 4:46–54

*. . . He went and begged him to come down and
heal his son, for he was at the point of death.*
JOHN 4:47

His tail and one leg protruded stiffly from the snow. Oh, dear. I walked over and picked him up: some kind of swallow. I put him under my arm inside my jacket. I have read of birds who appeared to be dead and then came back to life again by being placed under people's arms for a time. Maybe this would be one of them.

I pulled him out briefly to show Q. Maybe he's not dead, I said. I walked around the house with the bird under my arm for a little while. Nothing. But his eyes were open. So if he did come alive, he'd at least be able to see things. His little body was hard and cool in my hand, but it seemed that I felt it growing a little softer and warmer. I took him out again and looked at him. Nothing.

As interested as I was in this enterprise, I did have work to do. I carefully set the bird inside the fireplace screen to get the full benefit of the embers. Nice and warm, but not hot. I went upstairs to my office, back to work. Once in a while during the course of the afternoon I went down to check on the bird. He hadn't moved.

In the evening, I came downstairs, to be greeted by a roaring fire. What about the bird? I asked Q. *He's having a decent Christian cremation as we speak*, he said, pointing to the fire. I nodded. I would have been thrilled to feel the little heartbeat begin, to feel the tiny beginnings of movement in my hand. I would have been thrilled to see someone cross back over from seeming death. I have sat, many times, at the bedsides of people who have died, felt the awe of watching life leave its physical home, looked and seen that the body is still there but that it is now unoccupied, had the crazy wish that it could be started up again: All the parts are there, everything is there, could we not help her back into life? And then remembered that, somehow, life is more than its mechanics, than the presence of all the parts. That it comes—visits—for a season, and then it goes.

JANUARY 9

Pss 121, 122, 123 * 131, 132
Isaiah 63:1–5
Revelation 2:18–29
John 5:1–15

*"I have no one to put me into the pool . . . and while I am
making my way someone else steps down ahead of me."*
JOHN 5:7

Poor guy. Even going for healing was beyond him. Even there, the fittest got in first.

Some things are beyond us. Some things we used to be able to do. Other things we've never been able to do. Many of my powers are much less acute than they once were. I try and fail to do things that used to be easy. Panic attempts entrance, but I bar the doors successfully, no matter which one she tries. What if I don't finish this on time? What if I forgot something important? What if it's not good? *Well, then, you'll just fix it and get on with your life,* I answer with as maddening a calm as I can muster. *Did you really think you were so important that the world would come to a standstill without your work?*

I do my best, and it will have to be good enough. If you have resolved to do the same thing for twenty years in a row and never done it, then perhaps it's not in God's plan for you. And perhaps something else is, but you're so fixed on the grail of your unfulfilled ambition that you can't see it.

If you weren't trying to do what you can't do, what might you be doing instead? If you didn't do what you've always thought you were supposed to do, what would you do? Where is the path you have regarded with curiosity and never walked? And might it not be calling you now, inviting you to turn off the familiar road and go somewhere new?

What a frightening thought.

JANUARY 10

Pss 138, 139:1–17 (18–23) * 147
Isaiah 65:1–9
Revelation 3:1–6
John 6:1–14

I said, "Here I am, here I am," to a nation that did not call on my name. I held out my hands all day long to a rebellious people ..."
ISAIAH 65:1–2

But I'm your fiancée, the young woman wailed, pursuing her companion, grabbing onto his arm as he turned from her and attempted to walk away. Clearly we were witnessing the public airing of something we would all have been better not seeing, but sometimes a person just doesn't have privacy. Finally the young man slipped into the men's room, leaving his beloved weeping on the other side of the door.

He's not worth it, I wanted to tell her. *You can do better.* But I don't know that. I held my peace.

I don't know what their argument was about, but I do know that she was bringing the whole weight of their relationship to bear on it. God does this a lot in the Old Testament: He calls Israel to live up to the standard set by his love. Love ennobles us. Any love does that— any human love, and certainly the divine love. And it demands that our action toward the beloved partake of the nobility it confers on us. Demands it, in the name of the relationship itself. You can't treat me that way and say you love me. I'm your fiancée.

But I'm your Lord! How can you go on as if I were not? How can you act as if you did not know my law? You are only you because I am myself!

The heartbreak in the young woman's voice and demeanor was the same as God's heartbreak. *How could you? Don't you know who I am? And isn't who I am part of who you are?*

JANUARY 11

Pss 148, 150 * 91, 92
Isaiah 65:13–16
Revelation 3:7–13
John 6:15–27

A thousand may fall at your side, ten thousand at your right hand.
PSALM 91:7

This is not really a prediction of victory for the chosen. It is more of a wish. It is a blessing. It pictures the longed-for deliverance, and the vision is a prayer. *May this come to pass*, the singers must have thought as they sang it, perhaps immediately before the armies went into battle.

It pictures all the hazards of battle: the spears and arrows, of course, but also "the plague that stalks at mid-day." Things go wrong in war-torn places that don't have anything to do with shooting:

More soldiers died from the flu in World War I than from gunshot wounds. People starve in wars. Women and children are raped in wars. Buildings and whole cities are destroyed. The civilian water supply suffers and sometimes dries up. Refugees move out on their hazardous journeys to unwelcoming destinations. The elderly are left behind to die.

We have one life to live here on the earth. One childhood. One adolescence. We don't get a second chance at any of it. That is why it is such an enormity to send thousands of young people into battle, knowing that irreplaceable lives will be cut short.

Pray for those who do the sending. They, too, have lost their innocence forever, no matter how right their cause. The blood of a generation is on their hands, and they know this. None of them will be the ones who fight and die, and they know that, too. There is nothing fair about all this. And this they also know.

JANUARY 12, EVE OF I EPIPHANY

Pss 98, 99, (100) * 104
Isaiah 66:1–2, 22–23 * Isaiah 61:1–9
Revelation 3:14–22 * Galatians 3:23–29; 4:4–7
John 9:1–12, 35–38

You do not realize that you are wretched . . .
REVELATION 3:17

Something inconsequential about the arrangement of a few odd pieces of china in a kitchen cupboard, and I find myself in tears. Q is puzzled but patient. We can do this another time, he says. We don't have to do it now.

I am too distressed even to answer. *What is wrong with me?* I shriek silently as I climb the stairs. I acted like a moody teenage down there. I sit down at the computer in despair.

I never do ascertain what caused my weepy mood. In a little while, it has passed, and I am writing away on an essay that's not half bad. I am realizing that I like this, that I like my desk and my

candles, that I love to write and am now blessed with enough time
to do so.

It was a low seratonin level. Maybe it was too many carbohy-
drates, or too much caffeine. There is no wrong time of the month
for me any more, so it's not that. Nothing awful has happened to
me lately, or to anyone in my family.

So I guess it's just a bad mood.

What would we be without our moods? If we passed every day
in the same state of happy equilibrium? When I am down in the
dumps, I think it would be a fine thing not to have ups and downs.
And I wouldn't mind at all not being prone to depression. But still:
The ebb and flow of mood is one of the most human things about
us. We don't just respond to what is outside of us. We respond to
what is inside of us, too, an interior landscape full of mystery.

SUNDAY, EPIPHANY I

Pss 146, 147 * 111, 112, 113
Isaiah 40:1–11
Hebrews 1:1–12
John 1:1–7, 19–20, 29–34

All people are grass, their constancy is like the flower
of the field. The grass withers, the flower fades . . .
ISAIAH 40:6–7

The train up into Central New York takes me away from the coast
and whatever gentling effect it has on the weather. New York is a
big state, and most of it is a lot colder than Manhattan in the winter.

But here in the train it is warm, and the little towns whiz by, still
and frozen in the moment of my passing them by. There are people,
I know, who never leave their little towns, whose parents and grand-
parents are buried there. I envy them their stability. My parents'
graves are far from me. My childhood school. The woods behind
our house.

Actually, though, the woods aren't there anymore. They were cut down, and rows of houses come right up to our back fence now. So the people who stayed there don't have the woods, either, any more than I do. Nothing stayed the same for them, either. Nothing stays exactly the same for any of us.

Maybe that is what draws us to faith more than any other thing: our dismay at the way things pass away. My life runs through my fingers like water. I cannot hold it. That everything changes is a sign of that. *You don't live here anymore. This is no longer yours. It has forgotten you.*

And so we long for a place that does not change or go away. Where we are not forgotten.

God does not change. Or, perhaps, it is closer to the truth to say that God encompasses our changes. And so God doesn't go away. Everything else does, but God remains.

MONDAY IN EPIPHANY I

Pss 1, 2, 3 * 4, 7
Isaiah 40:12–23
Ephesians 1:1–14
Mark 1:1–13

Have you not known? Have you not heard?
Has it not been told you from the beginning?
ISAIAH 40:21

I cannot help but look blankly at my visitor: What is she doing here? As the truth dawns on me, my heart sinks: I've done it again. Gotten confused about a date. My pocket calendar helps me, but not enough. What I really need is a nurse.

My visitor takes it well, and we reschedule. I grab my bags and head for the station, where I will catch a train for—for where? Begins with a "u." Utrecht? No, Utica. I'm going to Utica.

What's your topic? Q asks as we ride along. He *would* have to ask. I don't know what my topic is. They told me, but I forgot.

Will it ever return, my missing memory? Or will life's narrative become increasingly slippery? Is it because I try to do too much, or is it just frailty? You're not supposed to get frail when you get old now; you're supposed to be athletic and raring to go right up until the moment you drop dead. I don't want to live to be 120, by the way, the way we're assured we can. It's just too much work.

Still, I comfort myself that my forgetfulness afflicts only the details of life: the names of people, places, and things. Appointments. I have not yet forgotten the things that matter: God loves the world and is worthy of any sacrifice I might find it within my power to make. That every human being is of infinite value. That we can usually do much more than we think we can. I have not forgotten those things.

TUESDAY IN EPIPHANY I

Pss 5, 6 * 10, 11
Isaiah 40:25–31
Ephesians 1:15–23
Mark 1:14–28

"What is this? A new teaching—with authority! He commands even the unclean spirits, and they obey him."
MARK 1:27

Ice lies on the Hudson River like junk, jagged slabs of it, piled willy-nilly on top of one another, strewn across a plain of milky white than extends halfway across the river, forming another hundred yards of coastline we didn't have last week. The water froze in mid-wave, forming dunes of ice on the river. A tanker glides north in the narrow corridor that remains navigable.

New York is New York because of this river. It would never have become the greatest city in the world were it not a seaport. I ride along its length, watching the city give way to the country. What was it like when Henry Hudson sailed upstream for the first time? Used to the densely inhabited shores of the Dutch waterways he knew best, he must have looked up in wonder at the high cliffs just beyond Manhattan, at the impenetrable forest. Had he known what immensities lay beyond them, that the land went on for three thousand miles and more, he might have doubted his own sanity.

The Dutch settlers in seventeenth-century New York invented tales about magical beings who lived in the mountains here in the new world. I can see why they did. This was a majestic, lonely place, a place unlike any other place they had been, a giant place where giants might live, where dwarves possessed magical powers, where anything might happen. Upstate is a place for lively imaginations.

In the nineteenth century, somebody's imagination ran away with him: an abandoned castle sits upon a small island in the middle of the river up near the Tappan Zee. The sky is visible through its empty gothic windows, and one wall has crumbled. Somebody tried to make a fairytale real.

But some imagination must remain in the mind. It can't all walk the earth. Reality is amazing enough without making things up. There aren't really giants. Dwarves aren't magical: They're normal people with a medical condition. And a castle in the middle of the Hudson? Fuggedaboudit.

WEDNESDAY IN EPIPHANY I

Pss 119:1–24 * 12, 13, 14
Isaiah 41:1–16
Ephesians 2:1–10
Mark 1:29–45

And he cured many who were sick with various diseases, and cast out many demons....
MARK 1:34

Without so much as backward glance, Q follows the doctor into the inner sanctum, leaving me in the waiting room. Don't know what I was expecting—a nervous look, a desire for reassurance. But Q doesn't look to me for reassurance. He expects to offer it, not receive it. And he's too old to change.

A friend told me that the procedure Q will have today is a painful one. I sat on that information for almost three weeks, even though it was given to me to pass on to my husband. I didn't want him to worry or be frightened.

Women are better at pain than men are, in my view. We have more of it, over a lifetime, and so it doesn't surprise us. Q has had very little—he has been spectacularly healthy throughout his life, always seeming younger than his actual age. In that, his life has been a charmed one. I don't want that to be over. Not that anybody asked me.

Not ten minutes passes before he returns. *Are you finished*, I ask, surprised. I had brought several hours worth of work with me, with which to pass the time. Why so soon? And why wasn't he ashen and trembling? Why wasn't the doctor hovering at his side, eager to talk to me and reassure me? Q strolled matter-of-factly toward the door. I got up and followed. I guess that was that.

We won't know the results of this procedure until two weeks from now. *Aren't you worried?* I ask Q.

No, he says. It makes no sense to worry about something before it happens.

That has never stopped me. Left to my own devices, my very prayer is apt to be a list of worries with an AMEN at the end. So possessed can I become with my own fears that I long ago concluded that a very wise way to pray about things that terrify me is to use no words at all. Just sit and wait for grace to touch me and calm me down, to touch the one for whom I pray, too. God knows what scares me. God knows why. I don't need to say a thing.

THURSDAY IN EPIPHANY I

Pss 18:1–20 * 18:21–50
Isaiah 41:17–29
Ephesians 2:11–22
Mark 2:1–12

*For he is our peace; in his flesh he has made both groups
into one and has broken down the dividing wall . . .*
EPHESIANS 2:14

Today, the Church around the world is much larger than the church in the Holy Land—only a tiny percentage of the people of modern Israel are Christian. But the work of the Anglican Church is large there: two hospitals, one in Gaza and one in Nablus in the West Bank. A clinic, a nursing home. One college and several intermediate schools, including one for the deaf and one for the education of girls. Vibrant churches and community centers, all struggling but flourishing in the midst of an increasingly violent and oppressive day-to-day situation.

We close our eyes and imagine Jesus, imagine the rocks by the river Jordan, imagine the old villages, the cobbled streets of Jerusalem. We imagine crowds of people in first-century dress. Donkey carts and camels. Ancient things. We open our eyes and see modern people running through those same old streets, hiding behind trash cans, dodging bullets, driving tanks into the side of a house and knocking the whole thing down. And beyond our vision, the stuff of daily life in almost impossible circumstances: A baby is born. A little girl stands patiently in her school uniform while her mother braids her hair. A classroom of deaf children talks, silently but a mile a minute, with their hands. A doctor leans closer to his patient and listens intently through his stethoscope.

Our faith was born there. All three of the Abrahamic faiths live there and have lived there for centuries. One of these days they will do so in peace, as difficult as that is for us to imagine now. It is possible that the tiny group of Christians in that beautiful and troubled place will be the key to this uniting, providing a third party in between the warring two who figure so prominently in the sad headlines we read every day.

Christians? Schools. Deaf children talking excitedly to their teachers. Brand new babies coming for their checkups. Old people sitting in the sun together. Young people in college and trade schools. There are worse associations a faith could have in a warring country than these lovely ones. Now we work in that holy and tragic land in a time of war. But everything we have there is something that will build the peace. When it comes, we will already be there, ready to embrace it.

FRIDAY IN EPIPHANY I

Pss 16, 17 * 22
Isaiah 42:(1–9) 10–17
Ephesians 3:1–13
Mark 2:13–22

*He will not cry or lift up his voice, or make it heard
in the street; a bruised reed he will not break,
and a dimly burning wick he will not quench . . .*
ISAIAH 42:2–3

*The Lord goes forth like a soldier, like a warrior he
stirs up his fury; he cries out, he shouts aloud . . .*
ISAIAH 42:13

A marked contrast, within a few verses of each another—the silence of the servant of God and the militant fury of God himself. The first is a faithful, patient, quiet friend of the poor. And the second? Don't get on his bad side.

Isaiah did not imagine it, but we envision those two figures as part of the same Trinity: God the Father and God the Son. We think the Servant is Jesus, because Jesus is our messiah, but Isaiah didn't know about Jesus. And we know that this identification is hard on some of us—on people like Peter, for instance, and perhaps on others among Jesus' friends who longed for a strong, even military messiah. Turns out they didn't know about Jesus, either, and they knew him personally.

But this Servant, though patient and tender with the suffering, is not a wimp. There is a courage that is not bombastic, a courage that bides its time, strives slowly and patiently against evil, doesn't give up and doesn't give in and eventually prevails. He will carry his cross on his own shoulders, submit to his own martyrdom. He will pause in the midst of it to heal a servant's severed ear, to reassure a convicted thief of God's love, to settle his mother's affairs. Nothing about what happens to him will speak of victory, not right away.

This patience is part of the victory. Not all victory is loud. Much of it is quiet and persistent. Not all victory is obvious, and some of it remains hidden for a long, long time.

SATURDAY IN EPIPHANY I

Pss 20, 21:1–7 (8–14) * 110:1–5 (6–7), 116, 117
Isaiah 43:1–13
Ephesians 3:14–21
Mark 2:23–3:6

For this reason I bow my knees before the Father, from whom every family in heaven and on earth takes its name.
EPHESIANS 3:14–15

Our church is just like a family: People always say about their parishes. A psychotherapist might pause at that—not everything about every family is life-giving. But what they mean is that their church is home: that they love each other, know about each other, care for each other.

The psychotherapist may have a point. Interestingly, Paul never referred to the church as a family. Paul doesn't say the church is like a family. He says it's like a body. It has members that depend on each other, regardless of how they may or may not be feeling. Each one affects all the others, for good or for ill.

Our priest is such a nurturing person, people sometimes say. But take a look at the ordination vows some time—they do not include a promise to nurture. A priest vows many things, but being everybody's mommy or daddy isn't one of them. Together, the church provides a place where people grow in understanding of God's ways with us, where they ask the hard questions and struggle for answers, where they subside into adoration at the beauty of the Lord. Such people will be better nurturers of those people whom it is their task to nurture for having taken the time to enter the house of God and nourish themselves.

Because it is God who is our Father. And—though there are fewer attestations to this in scriptures that come to us from a patriarchal world—our Mother, too. God nurtures without smothering, challenges without abusing, corrects every excess or deficit in the human adventure of growth and sends us out to live in the world, not as large children, but as loving, energetic adults.

SUNDAY, EPIPHANY II

Pss 148, 149, 150 * 114, 115
Isaiah 43:14–44:5
Hebrews 6:17–7:10
John 4:27–42

"Come and see a man who told me everything I have ever done."
JOHN 4:29

When they hear about his encounter with one of their more colorful neighbors at the town well, many of the Samaritans believe in Jesus because of the special effects: *He told me everything I have ever done!* People in the gospels are always impressed by Jesus' clairvoyance.

Jesus himself, however, puts little stock in it. He has a more urgent mission than fortune-telling, and when he strides into the middle of it and begins to preach the kingdom, people forget all about his ESP.

They are like us: Initially we, too, hope that Jesus will somehow help us beat the system. We'll stop losing, finally, and win for a change. We'll be prosperous because we believe. Our loved ones won't get sick, and neither will we. Our marriages won't end. We'll have no doubts and no troubles. We'll have no surprises.

When the Samaritans sit down and talk with Jesus, though, they forget about beating the system. He looks at them. He listens. He invites them deeper, and they follow where he leads. They look at this stranger and encounter the God who holds all our joy and sorrows in his hand.

Now they believe because of his word, they say. He has set their faith in motion. To believe is to follow. To believe is to act. To believe is to decide.

We spend a lifetime learning and relearning how to believe. Our self-absorption trips us up regularly. *Are you sure God is here?* we wail in one of life's terrible moments. *Then why does it hurt so much?*

Faith is about much more than coming out on top. Faith is about following Christ down some pretty rocky paths. Life in Christ remains a challenge for everyone. The Samaritan woman thought first of never having to lug heavy jugs of water home from the well. But that wasn't what the living water was. At first, she didn't get it. I imagine it dawned upon her slowly, the way it dawns on most of us.

MONDAY IN EPIPHANY II

Pss 25 * 9, 15
Isaiah 44:6–8, 21–23
Ephesians 4:1–16
Mark 3:7–19a

. . . we must grow up in every way . . .
EPHESIANS 4:15

From my window, I can see the trudge toward the school: kids with musical instruments in their bulky cases, kids wearing enormous backpacks—"What's *in* this thing?" their parents say, hefting the heavy bag—kids in pairs, kids alone. Kids happy to be going. Kids who don't want to go.

The school year seems to have gone on forever. And it will go on forever, too, stretching into the future with no end in sight. It feels like they've always been in the seventh grade and always will be. A sign in front of the high school says that eighth-grade parents are invited to an orientation, to see what high school will be like for their darlings. In case they've forgotten what high school is like.

If they remember, they know that it's hard. Not the work, the life. They remember that it takes a tough kid to withstand having worn the wrong shirt to school. Such a thing sticks to your reputation mercilessly and can stick to it for years. If ever an institution invited people to idolatry, it is the American high school. It prepares us for the practice of paranoia, invites us to measure ourselves by the standards of others, introduces us to the chimera of popularity and then snatches it cruelly out of our hands.

The best thing anybody can do for a young person is help him not take it too seriously. To remind her of the self that lives independently of what everybody else is saying and doing. To celebrate mightily whenever the courage to do that appears.

The men and women serving in the armed forces just left the world of high school, most of them. For most of them, this is their first time away from home. Most of them are just on the edge of the time of life when they can assert their own beauty and goodness, claim themselves on their own, by their own standards. I watch their younger brothers and sisters on their way to school—a year or two ago, that was them. Now they peer through telescopes, stare at instrument panels, practice with their rifles, run at a crouch through a training course with a forty-pound pack on their backs, the descendant of those heavy backpacks we used to wonder about. They used to sleep until noon, but most days they arise before dawn. They don't trudge now. They march. Their parents at home imagine them marching. *Is that really you?*

Dear God. Their youth fills us with fear. It breaks our hearts. Soldiers are young—younger than we realized when we were young, too. The hard-jawed infantrymen we remember are suddenly our own children, and it's almost more than we can bear.

TUESDAY IN EPIPHANY II

Pss 26, 28 * 36, 39
Isaiah 44:9–20
Ephesians 4:17–32
Mark 3:19b–35

"Who are my mother and my brothers?"
MARK 3:33

The lights were still on in many parts of the old farmhouse as I drove up, and my bathrobed hostess appeared in the doorway. It was pushing ten o'clock. Two dogs the size of loveseats sniffed at me until they were satisfied. "Bernese Mountain dogs," Ann said, as she carried my suitcase. "They're ours. My sister and her family moved in last week, though, and so now there's another dog and two more cats. I think there are five or six cats here now, so you'll be right at home."

Five or six cats is almost enough.

I was to sleep in the room of one of their daughters; judging by the poster on the wall, she left for college when the Spice Girls were still big. Some of her CDs are still here, a couple of elastic ponytail holders, pictures of her, eager and confident in her red soccer uniform; mugging with two high school friends; lovely in a white prom dress; arm in arm with her sister on another special-dress-day. College is far from here—Colorado. On the nightstand are some books about the Rocky Mountains.

Relatives and animals come and go as the need arises in this old house. In the morning, Ann's husband makes omelettes, then helps his little niece with her homework until it is time for another daughter's boyfriend to walk her to school. The niece is in the second grade. She goes to the same school their kids went to when they were little.

"My kids think the house should always be just the same," Ann laughs. "When they come back at Thanksgiving, I don't know what I'll do. I've got people in almost all the rooms." We think home should stay the same. We can change, but we don't want home to change. Don't want our parents to change. Want the place of childhood to remain, a refuge if we need it, from the difficult present, the encroaching future.

Of course, the place of all our childhoods does remain: There it is, intact, within us. Press the right button and you're five years old again. Press it again and you begin to act like it. All of what has made us remains locked within us, and sometimes it pops out again, asserting itself absurdly in the context of some adult situation where it sticks out like a sore thumb. "Oops," we say. "Sorry. That was childish of me."

Childlike is what we want to be, not childish. Full of trust, open to wonder, always interested in things, ready to love, eager to play. Secure at home. No matter where home is now.

WEDNESDAY IN EPIPHANY II

Pss 38 * 119:25–48
Isaiah 44:24–45:7
Ephesians 5:1–14
Mark 4:1–20

"Listen! A sower went out to sow."

MARK 4:3

A garden is so much like a church. So much care and feeding. Such competitiveness among the plants—some of them literally choke each other to death if you don't get out there and put a stop to it. The big gorgeous ones get lots of attention, but then one comes along that looks almost dead all season and suddenly, almost overnight, blooms splendidly forth. Never write anybody off completely. You just don't know.

Some of them can't grow where you try to put them. They need to move to where they can be more at home. That place may not even be in your garden—just because you want them doesn't mean yours is the best place for them. Sometimes you have to admit defeat and give them away.

In all the planting and husbandry, your role is so secondary. God is the main actor in a garden, and God's special relationship with each plant is so much more determinative of its life than anything you will do. You provide a comfortable place with the right light and the right soil and they do the rest. The will to grow and propagate is powerful in them, and they are good at it. God has endowed them with exactly the intelligence they need to keep their kind going.

And there's where the similarity ends. The goal of a plant is to perpetuate its kind. It will do whatever it must to accomplish that. People aren't plants, and a church isn't really a garden. Human beings can transcend our own needs for the good of others if we decide to do that. Some have actually given their lives to that end. Churches that exist solely for their own sakes ought more properly to be considered museums or social clubs.

And people who exist solely for their own needs, who never lift their eyes from their own plates?

They never bloom. And they just can't understand why.

THURSDAY IN EPIPHANY II

Pss 37:1–18 * 37:19–42
Isaiah 45:5–17
Ephesians 5:15–33
Mark 4:21–34

Wives, be subject to your husbands as you are to the Lord.
EPHESIANS 5:22

This is the passage nobody wants to read in church. The one they rib you about at coffee hour afterward, if you were the unlucky female lector who drew it. Wives dig their husband in the ribs and the men chuckle audibly. *Paul was a man of his time*, the curate begins bravely in her sermon, and the congregation settles back to watch her stew.

Poor thing. He *was* a man of his time, she's right. That's exactly our problem: We are people of *our* time. Not of Paul's. Every person of faith lives out his or her life in a particular time and place. It's never exactly the same for any two people. Scripture shows us snapshots of people in other eras doing what we must also do: figuring out how to live a faithful life in the setting in which we find ourselves.

It is not true that the people who were closer to Jesus in time—first-century people—were holier than we are. Proximity in time is not what made them holy. Those who were holy became so the same way we do, by being keenly alert to the mysterious signs of God's presence in their lives, by learning the hard way to set aside their self-absorption and fall in love with God. The life of faith is a life steeped in mystery. It has little to do with certainty.

Marriage, actually, is a good model for it. *Who is this?* you ask yourself, as you stare at your mate across the breakfast table. You've spent ten thousand mornings just like this one, sat here in the same two chairs, and suddenly it is as if you had never laid eyes on him. As if he were new. *Who is this?* You ask yourself again, and another day of discovery begins.

FRIDAY IN EPIPHANY II

Pss 31 * 35
Isaiah 45:18–25
Ephesians 6:1–9
Mark 4:35–41

Children, obey your parents . . . Slaves, obey your earthly masters.
EPHESIANS 6:1, 5

Masters and parents, don't be unreasonable. Be rational and kind. It's always striking, in reading ancient words, to see how matter-of-factly a writer deals with something that seems strange to a modern reader: It seems to Paul that the relationship between a master and a slave is like that between a parent and a child. And that a relationship between a master and slave can be a redemptive one. *No on both counts*, we would say. But it made sense at the time.

If those on the top rungs of a hierarchy are generous, the hierarchy will not be a painful one. But it will still be a hierarchy. If they are something other than kind, there is no protection within the system for the ones on the bottom. Their well-being is completely up to someone else. Not a safe place to be.

Blind obedience. Iron discipline. Absolute power. Human beings sometimes live within the matrix of these things. But the direction of history has been to move beyond them. We have traveled many miles on the path of personal dignity and autonomy since Paul wrote to the Ephesians. I can see the first steps of that long journey in his temporizing advice: You may have absolute power over someone else, but God is mightier than the mightiest human authority. Don't abuse the power you have. You have a master, too.

What looks to us like the anachronistic power arrangements of another age looked to those who first read these letters like a breath of liberating fresh air. Might won't be enough to make right? There will be obligations toward the weak? Even the ones we own, lock, stock, and barrel?

My goodness. I wonder what else might be in store.

Someday the things we assume will also look quaint to those who read about us. *How could they have tolerated that?* our descendents will ask each other in disbelief. They were Christians, and yet they grew fat while other people around the world dug through the garbage dumps for food. How could they have done that and not seen the contradiction?

How, indeed. It will be revealed in time.

⟍ SATURDAY IN EPIPHANY II

Pss 30, 32 * 42, 43
Isaiah 46:1–13
Ephesians 6:10–24
Mark 5:1–20

*"Go home to your friends, and tell them how
much the Lord has done for you . . ."*
MARK 5:19

I'm going to qualify at the meeting, my friend says. That means she will tell the story of her descent into the hell of addiction and her resurrection from it into sobriety.

She cannot tell it without weeping, and she doesn't try not to. She is not ashamed of her tears. *I've won every single one of them,* she says, *and they are tears of joy just as much as they are tears of pain. I don't know which one they are any more, joy or pain. I've had so much of both.*

She had no home. No family left, none who would speak to her anyway. Her health was a ruin. She had lost everything. She longed to die, living hurt so. She had no self left, it seemed. Just the desire for alcohol.

This must be what it was like for the Gerasene demoniac. No self left. Just the demon.

And yet, as far as the demoniac had traveled from ordinary human life, it was not so far that Jesus couldn't reach him. That Jesus couldn't bring him back. However much larger the demons were than he was, Jesus was bigger and stronger than either of them.

It is never too late, and you are never too far gone. No matter what. When human strength has given up on you, the divine strength is just getting warmed up. Just beginning to enfold you and lift you up.

Today she has a home. And an income. A host of friends, some of whom have been delivered as she has been delivered and some of whom don't know the first thing about any of that.

SUNDAY, EPIPHANY III

Pss 63:1–8 (9–11), 98 * 103
Isaiah 47:1–15
Hebrews 10:19–31
John 5:2–18

Therefore the Jews started persecuting Jesus, because he was doing such things on the sabbath. But Jesus answered them, "My Father is still working, and I also am working." For this reason the Jews were seeking all the more to kill him, because he was not only breaking the sabbath, but was also calling God his own Father, thereby making himself equal to God.

JOHN 5:16-18

Here we see religious authorities using the rules of the Sabbath against the Lord of the Sabbath. That's no good—it wasn't even considered good *then*. The Pharisees who advocated such rigor were considered fanatical by their own co-religionists. Jewish law already argued in favor of saving a life on the Sabbath. Or feeding an animal in your care. Healing wasn't outside the boundaries of permissible work. When Jesus told his disciples that the Sabbath was made for us, not we for the Sabbath, he was arguing right from his own scriptures, and it wasn't a shocking concept.

Very few of us are in danger of acting like those folks. We face the other danger: that there will be no Sabbath at all in our lives, that we will work and shop and drive and e-mail and pack it all into each day and never stop until it's filled to overflowing with our busyness. Those of us who remember Sunday blue laws remember that we managed somehow to survive without stores open every hour of every day of the week, that our Sabbath really did have a sleepy rhythm to it that was different from the rhythm of our other days.

Truth to tell, I remember sometimes hating it. I was a child, and I wanted things to happen. My parents were too quiet. There was nothing to do. I remember despairing as I watched them subside into their naps—I didn't know, then, how tired you could get from working all week. How much good a Sabbath could do.

But I was not too bored to realize how good it was that they were home. That we were together. That nobody had school or work. That this was just for us.

MONDAY IN EPIPHANY III

Pss 41, 52 * 44
Isaiah 48:1–11
Galatians 1:1–17
Mark 5:21–43

Immediately aware that power had gone forth from him, Jesus turned about in the crowd and said, "Who touched my clothes?"
MARK 5:30

I could not help but be moved: Here was St. Francis's simple brown robe, so old, so tattered. And his shoes. Clothing the saint had actually worn. This was in Asissi.

But I saw a similar set of clothing, said to have belonged to Francis, in another monastery in another hill town. And then another. *Uh-oh.* How many suits of clothing did Francis have? He was famous for his austerity, even in those austere times.

Q smiled at my disappointment, at how important it was to me that these be the very clothes Francis had worn. But it felt to me that they must surely have a special power, that touching something that had touched the saint must surely give to me a molecule of some kind of power I lacked before.

I could not have touched them, anyhow, no matter whose they were. They were behind a plate of thick glass in a locked display case. We could only look at them and imagine the saint wearing them, picure him: small, he must have been. Much smaller than I am.

We live in physical bodies, and so physical bodies are important to us. The power we know best is physical power. The healing we crave is physical healing.

And Christ, through whom the world is created, is the Lord of all this physicality. Partook of it himself, really living, really dying. Really healing, even now, so long after he walked the earth. Knew tiredness and loss of power, this Christ in whom the power of creation and restoration lived. Lives.

I return home from a retreat. It was a good one, but I am tired from it, too tired to eat supper. Horizontality is all I crave. I slip in between the sheets of our bed and feel my bones sag into it. *Ah.* My part of Christ's work of creation and restoration, modest though it is, takes a lot out of me, too.

We walk in his footsteps. Wear his clothing, in a design appropriate to our era, not to his. Sometimes he was wearied by his work. Ours wearies us, too. Even in this, we are in his image.

TUESDAY IN EPIPHANY III

Pss 45 * 47, 48
Isaiah 48:12–21
Galatians 1:18–2:10
Mark 6:1–13

"Is not this the carpenter, the son of Mary and brother
of James and Joses and Judas and Simon, and are not his
sisters here with us?" And they took offense at him.

MARK 6:3

This place, Nazareth, is the place where Jesus was a teenager. He grew up here and they know his folks. This is his synagogue. They knew him when he was fourteen, and fifteen, and seventeen. Of course, those ages meant something different in those days: To us, seventeen is still a kid, but to them, it was a grown man. Still, whenever the awkward years of adolescence were in those days, those people saw them in Jesus.

I hope your teenaged years were the best time of your life, like people always say they are. But maybe they weren't. Maybe they were just awful: times when you didn't ever know what to do, when everything you did seemed to make you look stupid, when you were embarrassed almost all the time. When everyone but you seemed poised and self-confident, when everyone but you seemed to have love in life, to have a boyfriend or a girlfriend, to be popular. When you were too tall or too short, too fat, too skinny, flat on top when all the other girls were curvaceous, still a treble when all the other guys were manly baritones, not mature-looking, when everyone else looked like a movie star. Everyone. When you fought with your parents, and really believed sometimes that they didn't love you, that all they wanted was to keep you from having any fun. When you wanted desperately to be free, but didn't have any money of your own, or a job or a car or any choice but to live where people didn't understand you or value you. Trapped. Your parents had to take you places because you couldn't take yourself. You were a prisoner.

Jesus comes to preach deliverance in the place where he was a teenager. Maybe he knew something about needing deliverance. I know we think he was unnaturally good as a child and didn't cry when he was a baby, but another scenario is possible: Perhaps his life was a struggle, like ours. Perhaps it was hard, coming to terms with who he was. Perhaps his parents didn't understand him—there is a glimmer of that in the scolding his mother gives him when he is twelve. Perhaps his contemporaries didn't understand him, either. We certainly don't. Perhaps growing up was hard for Jesus.

To think that might be true brings tears to my eyes, even after all these years. It was hard for me. I wouldn't be young again for a million dollars. Not for a billion. It is hard now, for some of the young people I love. Hard. Scary. Angry-making. Is it possible that Christ knows all about this pain? Is it possible that he has experienced it? That the crosses teenagers carry are known in the cross Jesus carries? If that is true, I will kneel at the foot of the cross and bathe it with my tears. Mine and the tears of all the kids I know who don't want anyone to see them cry.

WEDNESDAY IN EPIPHANY III

Pss 119:49–72 * 49, (53)
Isaiah 49:1–12
Galatians 2:11–21
Mark 6:13–29

*"I want you to give me at once the head
of John the Baptizer on a platter."*
MARK 6:25

It was a Halloween party at seminary, I believe. Or maybe it was Mardi Gras. Costumes, anyway: Wally and I went as Lent, in purple copes he designed and I made. Dan and Bob went as corpses. Reid went as Caligula, I think, and Dierdre, who was very beautiful, was some kind of nineteenth-century chorus girl. Paul was there, in a genuine Canterbury cap.

I think Cathy Grisham was Salome, but the hit of the evening was her husband Lowell, who was John the Baptist. Lowell was a very special John the Baptist: not the usual hairy-guy-in-burlap-with-a-bag-of-suspicious-looking-chocolate-candies John the Baptist, but *just the head*: Lowell's head protruded through a cardboard platter covered with tinfoil, which rested on his shoulders. The head was everything—he just wore a black cassock, because nobody was looking at anything below the neck. It was a wonderful costume. Perfect.

That was a peculiar time in the history of those young people studying for ministry. We knew how awesome a burden we were assuming, and we were not always sure we were up to it. And so we partied hard, too hard, some of us, as if to distract ourselves from the awesomeness of what we were about to do. And we assumed a studied outrageousness, sometimes, with regard to sacred texts. Made jokes about them. Laughed at them.

And then we graduated and went into the business of preaching those sacred texts to the world in which we found ourselves. It was an even more awesome task than we had suspected, and we were even less up to it than we knew. But God was even greater than any of us had dreamed. He took us, in all our silliness, and made us presentable, working in us more and more of what he needed us to be.

⟍ THURSDAY IN EPIPHANY III

Pss 50 * (59, 60) or 118
Isaiah 49:13–23
Galatians 3:1–14
Mark 6:30–46

And all ate and were filled; and they took up twelve
baskets full of broken pieces and of the fish.
MARK 6:42–43

Odd: snow or no, I know spring is coming. I can feel it. In a month, maybe sooner, the crocuses will be up. I have dog-eared the seed catalogue until at last I am ready, and today I will order too many seeds, which will annoy Q, a measured man who will never understand the value of having more than enough, just in case.

I overdo everything, and it troubles him. I serve him too much food, use too much soap, make too much tea. *Can't you just take what you need?* I suppose I could. But how would I know for sure, in advance, what that might be?

To me, overdoing everything is the imitation of Christ. The stuff of creation, spilling over the sides of whatever seeks to contain it and all over the floor. Way too much. There is never just the right amount of grace. It is not measured. It is not sensible. There is more than enough. It is free and abundant.

It is free and abundant because life is hard. Many things are born because many things die. Grace runs in a hard, strong current through human life because human life is uncertain: We never know when we're going to need an extra helping right now. We can never plan for our uncertain needs. But God does.

A female Downy Woodpecker appears at the feeder outside my office window. The birds have been ignoring this feeder for several months—it is on the northeast side of the house, and it's colder over here. They prefer the sunny southwest, where the other feeders are. Maybe I should just take it down until the weather warms up, I have thought more than once.

But if I had, the little lady woodpecker who happened by in a blizzard wouldn't have found it. I predict that she will stick close to the tree all day, hopping on and off the feeder, out of the worst of the wind.

You never know when the foolish things you do will have a purpose that mirrors the divine grace. You wouldn't want to miss that.

FRIDAY IN EPIPHANY III

Pss 40, 54 * 51
Isaiah 50:1–11
Galatians 3:15–22
Mark 6:47–56

The Lord God has given me the tongue of a teacher, that I may know how to sustain the weary with a word. Morning by morning he wakens—wakens my ear to listen as those who are taught.

ISAIAH 50:4

My daughter is a teacher. Another daughter is in training to become one. My husband is a teacher. My parents were teachers. I am a teacher. And yet I read these words with something of a start: So *that's* what a teacher does—she *sustains*. With words.

I have always thought a parent was primarily a teacher—you begin as soon as they're born, preparing them to make it without you. Your main job is to be sure they'll be okay when you're not around any more. If that sounds cold, it isn't: The main way people are okay is by becoming people who draw other people to them, and the main way they become such people is by having parents who teach love above all else. Anybody can learn to make a *béchamel* sauce—and if you don't, you can always just order out—but you need years of solid, joyful presence to become loving.

While they're learning all the other things they'll need to know—algebra, how to write a letter, how to make a web site, how to drive, how to get dumped by your girlfriend and survive it—the teacher sustains them. These lessons are wearying. Life is hard. *You can do it*, says the teacher. *Let's try again.*

Patience. The ability to look at old things with new eyes. A memory of what it was not to know. A desire to share the power of knowing. A respect for the process of learning itself. A willingness to let people take the time it takes to learn, the courage not to rush in and do it yourself, no matter how scary the failed attempts are to behold.

SATURDAY IN EPIPHANY III

Pss 55 * 138,139:1–17 (18–23)
Isaiah 51:1–8
Galatians 3:23–29
Mark 7:1–23

"There is nothing outside a person that by going in can defile, but the things that come out are what defile."
MARK 7:15

My shoes could use a polish—winter walking in the city is hard on them. I realize, though, as I tick off my options, that almost all the shoe-shines in New York are gone. There used to be a row of men along the fence opposite the Port Authority. Gone. The fence is gone, too. There used to be a man in front of Penn Station at the 8th Avenue entrance. There used to be several in front of Trinity Church. Not any more. Not since the bombing of the World Trade Center.

What do people do with their dirty shoes now—throw them away? At one time, you could make a living shining shoes in New York City. Not a big one, but a living. A rag and a brush and two tins of wax, and you would eat that day.

Jobs caring for people's feet are low in status, as if people's feet and shoes were unclean. But there is no such thing as menial work: One person has a need and another makes a business of meeting it. Money is exchanged and each is satisfied. The relative status of any part of human life plays no role in any of this. We made that part up.

The Bible is full of business. The prophets talk a lot about business ethics, about treating workers fairly and honestly, about buying and selling honestly. There is little support in scripture for the notion that faith and ordinary things have nothing to do with each other. And none for a haughty disdain for honest work.

SUNDAY, EPIPHANY IV

Pss 24, 29 * 8, 84
Isaiah 51:9–16
Hebrews 11:8–16
John 7:14–31

*". . . are you angry with me because I healed
a man's whole body on the sabbath?"*

JOHN 7:23

That was stupid, going outside in a blizzard with a tin of birdseed for the feeder, wearing only a bathrobe and slippers. I would only be a second, I thought as I opened the door and slipped out. I do it all the time. And it did only take a second to feed the birds. But the snow is a foot deep. It only took a second for it to fill the space between my bare feet and the shearling lining of the slippers. Ugh. Now the slippers are upside down over the heating vent.

I love the way this part of the world paralyzes itself over a snowstorm. In Minnesota, they don't. You have to be game out there. You have to get everywhere. Schools never close—once in a blue moon. They couldn't: Kids would never get an education if they did. And you're not really allowed to complain about it. You'd look foolish out there, griping about something as omnipresent as snow.

Happily, it is not so with us. We can treat a heavy snow as a state emergency: The governor of New Jersey did that this morning, along with governors of several other states. We can declare a snow

Sabbath, cancel things. Accept the gift of an extra day that falls into our laps like it's leap year. And, if we are what the radio calls "essential personnel," we can bask in the more rugged comfort of that status: We are essential. Brave. Well nigh indispensable. Able to leap tall buildings at a single bound. We can stomp into the places that need us so desperately in our heavy boots, cheerful and strong, heedless of the weather. Essential.

Jesus must have been essential personnel. Jesus did essential things on the Sabbath, life and death things. And kept his Sabbath— and his life—clear of nonessential things. It was easy for details to assume life and death significance that was not theirs, as easy then as it is now. Resist it. You know what's important. *Do not judge by appearances, but judge with right judgment.*

MONDAY IN EPIPHANY IV

Pss 56, 57, (58) * 64, 65
Isaiah 51:17–23
Galatians 4:1–11
Mark 7:24–37

"For saying that, you may go—the demon has left your daughter."
MARK 7:29

For saying what? I think it was for scolding him, because that is what the Syro-Phoenician woman did. Jesus was rude to her, and she called him on it. And he realized that he'd been bad-tempered for no good reason, and thought better of it. And then he fixed it.

This is not the way we usually think of Jesus, I know. For some reason, it's always been hard for us to go anywhere near the idea that his behavior on earth was not always perfect—although we affirm every week in the creed that he was fully human and fully divine. *Yet without sin*, someone will say, glaring at you pointedly, if you happen to suggest such a thing. But being without sin is not the same as being without error. *To err is human*, we say.

And to forgive, divine, goes the rest of the couplet. The redeeming love of Christ forgives all sin and makes it right. It gives us a place to run with it, to repair the world, if we have to. But it doesn't produce a place in which nothing ever goes wrong. In which people don't make mistakes. That's not what redemption is.

Out of our desire to honor God and praise the goodness of God, we shrink from the fullness of what incarnation really means. From its inherent contradiction. There was a reason that the Greeks couldn't believe in a God incarnate, and the reason was that it didn't make any sense. For sense, you must go elsewhere. What we have is scandal, outrageous mystery in which the mighty God lives the life of the powerless. This is what it means for God to have cast his lot in with us, to live in our world of risk and imperfection. To take on flesh that was really frail, not flesh pretending to be frail.

How was your day, one of his friends might have asked him at dinner that day. *Well, you know, there was this lady*, he might have begun, shaking his head ruefully.

TUESDAY IN EPIPHANY IV

Pss 61, 62 * 68:1–20 (21–23) 24–36
Isaiah 52:1–12
Galatians 4:12–20
Mark 8:1–10

I wish I were present with you now and could
change my tone, for I am perplexed about you.
GALATIANS 4:20

A long-distance relationship is hard. Letters help, of course, and e-mail. And you can always rack up huge telephone bills in the name of love. But there is no substitute for the ongoing ordinariness of day-to-day presence. We don't really know each other if we don't live together.

But a day-to-day relationship is hard, too. Love may be immense and genuine, but that doesn't mean it is not also a pain in the *derriere* at times.

That was certainly true of the love between Paul and his various churches. It is a testimony to the commitment the biblical writers had to keeping a complete record of the church's early life that they included as many letters of Paul as they did, because some of Paul's letters are not very friendly. They are old documents, now, and we read them as liturgy today, not with the immediacy with which they were read when they were received. If we did, we'd notice that many of them are long-distance scoldings.

This should help us be a little gentler with ourselves. They had a hard time with each other, too, those people who lived so long ago. They argued about things that mattered to them, too, as we do. They didn't agree about important matters of the faith, either.

Don't let anybody tell you that disagreement is proof that something's wrong. We don't know that. Sometimes it's a sign that something's right. Right enough to engage us with one another in sharp debate, because we trust each other enough to be honest about what really matters. This sharpness is not the opposite of love: The opposite of love is apathy. If we care enough to get hot under the collar, we care enough to work things out, no matter what it takes.

WEDNESDAY IN EPIPHANY IV

Pss 72 * 119:73–96
Isaiah 54:1–10 (11–17)
Galatians 4:21–31
Mark 8:11–26

Do not fear, for you will not be ashamed;
do not be discouraged, for you will not suffer disgrace;
for you will forget the shame of your youth . . .

ISAIAH 54:4

On the radio, they're playing the Supremes. I am singing, like Flo and Mary behind Diana Ross: "Ooooh . . ." I sing and hold the note, one hand on the steering wheel and one hand pointing up at the rearview mirror. Just like the Supremes, only old.

Madeline knows these songs, too—everybody knows the Supremes —but she doesn't sing along. She rolls her eyes at my performance and wonders quietly if she will die of embarrassment at my ungrand-motherly behavior.

Except she is smiling a little, behind her facade of ennui. *You're a dork*, she says. Yes, I suppose I am a dork. But I am your dork. Every-body gets to be embarrassed by their parents. We were. It's part of life and builds character. You're extremely blessed to have a grand-mother nearby. You get to be embarrassed that much more.

She has other things on her mind besides her embarrassing grand-mother, in any case. She starts high school tomorrow. In the car, a cell phone conversation about what will be worn on the first day. Later in the evening, a precise exchange about what time I should pick her up in the morning, so that we have time to go and get her friend and they can face the first day of the new school together.

Full of excitement and fear, self-confidence and self-doubt jock-eying for position within her tender spirit, exquisitely beautiful and not yet aware that this is so, she dresses carefully for this walk into her future. She is a scholar, too, as well as a young girl, and I think she is excited about the new work she will undertake at the new school. When she leaves it, four short years from now, it will be to leave us.

The four years stretch out in front of her—forever. I watch her as she enters the school building—"Don't call out to me or say anything dorky to me once I'm out of the car, Mamo, like 'good luck' or anything loud, okay?"—and I know that the four years will be over in what seems like ten minutes.

I won't say anything. Not a word. Not what a pretty baby you were. Not that I'm proud of you. Not that it's a delight to see your mother in you and your sister, little snippets of her here and there. I won't say that I know you will do well in high school. The last thing I will say to you—before you open the car door, so nobody hears and finds out that your grandmother is a dork—is that I am saying a special prayer for you today.

THURSDAY IN EPIPHANY IV

Pss (70), 71 * 74
Isaiah 55:1–13
Galatians 5:1–15
Mark 8:27–9:1

Then he began to teach them that the Son of Man must undergo great suffering, and be rejected by the elders, the chief priests, and the scribes, and be killed, and after three days rise again. He said all this quite openly. And Peter took him aside and began to rebuke him.

MARK 8:31–32

I sprint up the steep stairs to the train platform, blessing my angioplasty with every stride, just as the train pulls in. The platform is crowded: This express train is popular. I resign myself to standing all the way to New York. But lo, there are plenty of seats. Good.

In the morning, the train is quiet. Lots of cell phone jollity on the way home from work, but the early morning train is a contemplative place. People read their newspapers or stare silently out the window as the buildings whiz by. Many people sleep. I get out my little prayer book and say Morning Prayer—I got a late start this morning and didn't say it before writing the eMo, as I usually do.

The train is a good place to pray. The motion itself is oddly conducive to prayer: It is so mechanical, so out of our hands. And the awful fluorescent lighting seems bright and safe in the morning, as the grey sky pinks along the horizon and the day begins.

The New York City skyline is to our right as we approach the Hudson River. It is wounded now, of course: The twin towers of the World Trade Center used to get pink first, and the color worked its way up their immense sides as the sun rose, turning both surfaces golden. "Well, how very odd!" I remember thinking as I watched them burn. I was unable to grasp what was happening. Minimized it at the very moment I saw it with my own eyes. Rejected the possibility of what I saw. "Gosh, that looks like some fire. I hope nobody's hurt."

I can't believe I thought this, but I did. Saw the two of them smoking away like two chimneys and thought to myself that everybody must have escaped.

"I'm sure they got everybody out." *Sweet Jesus.*

We were all much younger then.

FRIDAY IN EPIPHANY IV

Pss 69:1–23 (24–30) 31–38 * 73
Isaiah 56:1–8
Galatians 5:16–24
Mark 9:2–13

*Jesus took with him Peter and James and John, and led
them up a high mountain apart, by themselves.*
MARK 9:2

The sunrise up here in the Adirondacks is spectacular, a friend writes. We exchange greetings each day after Morning Prayer, and she couldn't resist a word of praise for God's artistry.

I wish I could see it, I write back, but I am imagining being struck by it: The kiss of pink on the tops of the mountain, changing more and more into gold, the first rim of the round sun. Ah.

One important difference between the Old Testament and the New: Apart from the words of Jesus himself, there is little mention of nature in the New Testament. Never does anyone sit and look at a sunset and make up a song about it, like the psalmists do. Nobody enumerates animals and plants, like the author of Genesis. Once in awhile Jesus uses an agrarian metaphor, or one about the weather. But, except for considering the lilies of the field, even he never invites us simply to marvel at the loveliness of things. The New Testament is not a book about nature.

And Christians, as a result, have always been a little nervous about it. Suspicious. A little too proud of not having "nature gods," as it has been dismissively put. Especially the early Christians, the ones who wrote down what we have received as the New Testament. As if nature were a matter for lesser minds, while we smart folk are focused on heaven. No time for sunsets. Never mind the flowers. God is not there. God is in heaven. All this is passing away.

And it *is* all passing away. But that doesn't mean God is not there. We are set among things that are passing away, and God walks the earth with us, ephemeral or no.

This is why we read the psalms every day. They aren't self-consciously theological. They're just observant. They compare people to trees and fruit, find personality in the waves of the sea, watch a storm and feel its power. When Jesus does this, he echoes the psalms. Often, he quotes them directly. And, when Jesus wants his friends to see who he really is, he takes them up on a mountain. There, he is transformed, struck and changed, and his friends see it. It's one of those moments. They are struck and changed, too, for having seen it.

SATURDAY IN EPIPHANY IV

Pss 75, 76 * 23, 27
Isaiah 57:3–13
Galatians 5:25–6:10
Mark 9:14–29

Bear one another's burdens, and in this way you will fulfill the law of Christ . . . All must test their own work; then that work, rather than their neighbor's work, will become a cause for pride.

GALATIANS 6:2, 4

Bear one another's burdens. Okay. But everyone must test himself. Are both true? Can I do both? And which comes first, the self-sacrifice or the self-knowledge?

A woman comes to see me for the first time. She is reluctant to pray for herself. *It seems awfully selfish,* she says, *when I have so many blessings, and so many other people in the world have such difficult lives. Why should I bother God with my little problems?*

But such a concern rests on what is probably a mistake: God is not an overworked CEO with too much on his plate. God's love is limitless. Not a sparrow falls but God sees, we read in scripture. There is enough of God for you and for me.

Moreover, this becoming unselfishness may mask something a little less attractive: Maybe I don't want to pray for myself because I am unwilling to admit my weakness and neediness before God. Maybe I still think I'm the boss of everything in my life. Maybe I still think I'm alone. Maybe I am—secretly—my own God.

So pray for yourself first. If it makes you feel better not to ask for anything, don't. What you say isn't nearly as important as we all think it is. Just picture yourself in the open hands of God and contemplate the image. Because in the hand of God is exactly where you are.

You contemplate yourself and God at the same time in such a prayer. In such a prayer, you know, insofar as a human being can, as you are known. That is the time, after such location of your self within the love of God, that you can set out in the service of someone else.

SUNDAY, EPIPHANY V

Pss 93, 96 * 34
Isaiah 57:14–21
Hebrews 12:1–6
John 7:37–46

"Out of the believer's heart shall flow rivers of living water."
JOHN 7:38

It has been helpful to me to imagine the love of God as something like a river: mighty, strong, clean and cool, its current swift, carrying everything before it. It has been easy to imagine myself in that river, carried rapidly along. This is one of the ways in which I pray for myself. And one of the ways in which I pray for someone else.

Especially someone for whom I find it difficult to pray. Sometimes I need to pray for someone with whom I am angry. Or for whom I am afraid. Sometimes strong emotion on my part makes me tongue-tied—I don't know what to say that will not highjack me into an emotional U-turn away from where I want to go. In those moments, the river of God's love is a fine place for me to be. No words are necessary—God is certainly strong enough to know without my supplying appropriate wording.

It's good to have more than one way of praying. That way, you've got a spare if, for some reason or for no reason, your prayer gets stuck. Don't worry if you get stuck—just turn the page and do it another way. If Morning Prayer gets stuck, switch to Evening. Change books, if you use a book. Begin praying outside. Pray while exercising or while grooming the dog—both the dog and your loving care of him are good images for the unconditional love of God. Pray while ironing, and consider how the wrinkles smooth right out under the steamy discipline of the iron. Pray while cooking, meditating on all the ways in which you've been nourished in your life, sending life-giving nourishment to those for whom you offer your intentions.

You can do it anywhere. There is no end to the ways. The river of God's love is mightier than we can imagine and deeper than a human being can ever go.

MONDAY IN EPIPHANY V

Pss 80 * 77, (79)
Isaiah 58:1–12
Galatians 6:11–18
Mark 9:30–41

*If you offer your food to the hungry and satisfy the needs
of the afflicted, then your light shall rise in the
darkness and your gloom be like the noonday.*

ISAIAH 58:10

Damn. I've spilled tea all over my nice trousers. They are a neutral grayish color, so I suppose I could take a chance that the tea won't show. But tea is a force to be reckoned with: Once it's dry, it's there forever. They use tea as a dye.

I pick up some snow and begin to scrub. The friction of my scrubbing melts it, and soon the tea on my trousers is adequately diluted. Another crisis averted. Of course, now my fingers sting from the cold of my prolonged contact with the melting snow, but that will pass.

Maybe tea doesn't want to be a commuter drink. Maybe tea wants to be sipped from a china cup in a warm and pretty room, where there's plenty of time to appreciate it. Tea stains are unforgiving: Maybe that's a moral—"Now see here, young lady, you just sit yourself down and take it easy!"

Only women pick tea leaves in India. They are out in the early morning, bent double over the plants, large cloth sacks slung over their backs to receive the tiny leaves, their bright saris shading their faces from the hot sun. They pick all day, all season. And then they go home and cook supper for their large families.

I do not know if they drink tea themselves, the tea pickers. Many people in India do drink it, but I don't know about them. If they sit still, like ladies. If they use a china cup.

TUESDAY IN EPIPHANY V

Pss 78:1–39 * 78:40–72
Isaiah 59:1–15a
2 Timothy 1:1–14
Mark 9:42–50

We grope like the blind along a wall,
groping like those who have no eyes. . . .
ISAIAH 59:10

I am still shuffling books when the bell rings, signaling the beginning of the Evening Office. It is the Angelus: three sets of three rings for our silent *Aves*, followed by a steady nine for the collect. As the last tone dies away, the sisters begin the ancient words.

They have more books for their recitation of the Office than I use at home. I have one office book; they have an office book and a hymnal and a couple of others. Guests are given careful but intricately written instructions for finding everything, but it's still not easy, and I've been coming here for a long time.

That's okay. Everything doesn't have to be easy. Don't sing difficult music, experts in church growth say, and don't use funny church words to refer to things. People will be intimidated. And I guess there's plenty of truth in that: There needs to be a low threshold so that people will have the confidence to take that first step.

I observe, however, that it isn't always true that a newcomer can handle only vanilla. Some of them seem able to deal with Maple Walnut or Boysenberry Cream. Some people are intrigued by the mystery of the arcane words, the ritual not immediately crystal clear in its meaning. Some lean forward in their seats, eager to see and experience it. Some don't mind getting lost a bit; they subside into listening to the music and the words, letting the liturgy carry them for a while.

We in the twenty-first century are an impatient lot. We want to understand everything perfectly right away. But some of the loveliest things, the most important things, are things into which we must grow. And some people don't mind a little mystery at first. There is, after all, lots and lots of mystery later on.

WEDNESDAY IN EPIPHANY V

Pss 119:97–120 * 81, 82
Isaiah 59:15b–21
2 Timothy 1:15–2:13
Mark 10:1–16

*"Because of your hardness of heart he
wrote this commandment for you."*

MARK 10:5

A tough teaching about divorce, followed by a vision dear to many hearts: Jesus welcoming the children whom the disciples tried to shoo away. Something about adults and something about children. About things falling apart and people coming together.

You still meet people who think they can't receive communion in an Episcopal church because they've been divorced and remarried. You even meet other people who believe they still shouldn't. It's hard when moral teaching changes. What can we hold onto, if the rules change?

But the rules do change sometimes. Our Old Testament forbears lived in polygamous marriages. They held slaves and disposed of their slaves' sexual lives and even their children in ways that we would never countenance today. Life develops, and moral development is part of life's development. We are part of it. We can't sit this one out, in the dance of history. We have to dance every dance they play.

I often complain to myself—and sometimes to others—about the way things have changed since I was young. *You sound like your parents*, I tell myself, if I happen to really hear myself. They are gone now. Now I'm the one nostalgic for the way things used to be.

Some of us think things have gotten better. More inclusive. Kinder. Others think things have gotten too loose: Where is the commitment we used to take for granted? The stability?

Probably both are true. We are kinder now, more able to listen to new things. And we have lost stability, it's true. So what now? Do we abandon everything that has happened since, say, 1850? 1950? 478? Or do we give up on the past and set ourselves completely free from it?

Neither. We can't do either of those things. We're stuck with history, and we're headed inexorably into the future. Look and listen for the signs of the new, and be as well versed in your history as you possibly can—you'll need every second of it.

THURSDAY IN EPIPHANY V

Pss (83) or 146, 147 * 85, 86
Isaiah 60:1–17
2 Timothy 2:14–26
Mark 10:17–31

*And the Lord's servant must not be quarrelsome
but kindly to everyone, an apt teacher, patient,
correcting opponents with gentleness.*
2 TIMOTHY 2:24–25

Look, Q says, handing me the newspaper. It's a picture of two penguins kissing each other. *That's so cute*, I say. Further down the page is a picture of two monkeys lounging casually against each other, like a couple at the beach.

They're both boys, Q says, showing me the article. It's entitled "Love That Dares Not Squeak Its Name."

What's-Her-Name and Gypsy are both girl cats. They're very close as well: What's-Her-Name teaches Gypsy to hunt, and I saw them kiss once, at the bottom of the stairs. I'm all for anyone, of either gender, who can exert a civilizing influence on What's-Her-Name.

So same-sex courting behavior happens among animals, it seems. One pair of male penguins even hatched an egg—they so longed for a baby that they tried to hatch a rock, taking turns holding it next to their tummies, where penguin eggs are kept warm. So their human friend took pity on them and gave them a fertilized egg: They turned out to be model penguin parents. Sweet.

That's interesting, in view of all the noise about how unnatural and dangerous such things are among humans. IT'S NOT NORMAL!!! people say, truly frightened by it, and I suppose that's true: "Normal" is a statistical term, not a moral one, referencing the behavior of the majority of a population, and same-sex courting is a minority behavior. Something may or may not be normal. We still must make a judgment about whether or not it is good.

So maybe it's *not* unnatural. Maybe animals are gay sometimes, too. Does that mean it's fine for humans? Not necessarily, but not necessarily *not*, either. We are simply not going to get out of this controversy without rendering a judgment—a judgment based, not on statistics and not on animal behavior and not on a biased reading of select scripture passages and not on whether or not our friends disagree with it or our parents warned us against it, but on our own capacity to reason with intellectual rigor, and our own capacity to love and listen. That's what we do. We pursue the good things of life as God gives us wisdom to pursue them. We spend the energy we have on the world in which we live. Those of us who care to try to make it a better world. It need not be a homogeneous one.

FRIDAY IN EPIPHANY V

Pss 88 * 91, 92
Isaiah 61:1–9
2 Timothy 3:1–17
Mark 10:32–45

*For among them are those who make their way into
households and captivate silly women, overwhelmed by their
sins and swayed by all kinds of desires, who are always being
instructed and can never arrive at a knowledge of the truth.*

2 TIMOTHY 3:6–7

Read this! someone says to me, putting a copy of the latest pink-clouds-and-past-lives best seller into my hands. I am careful to make no promises. And it is by no means just women who rise to the bait.

Read this first! I wish I could counter, holding a Bible aloft. Why people will drink eagerly at everybody else's well when they haven't touched their own is a mystery. Or is it?

Scripture can be hard to read. Some of it—most of it—is not clear in meaning. It was written long ago, in cultures very different from ours. You have to look things up, learn about what ideas were in the air when these things were written. It's a lot of work.

But it's good work. There comes a time when you need to get off the bus: Settle on something into which you are willing to go deeply. Something worth marrying. Something to which you are willing to entrust all your future growth. There comes a time when you must commit. If you cannot arrive at this time, you remain a child. That must be what Paul meant by the "silly women."

It doesn't mean you'll have no further questions. Or that there won't always be new things to learn, or that there will be no contradictions in your life and belief. But everything can't be up for grabs forever, not if it's a life of spiritual depth you want.

Well, what if I choose the wrong thing? I say don't worry. If it's wrong, it will not satisfy you. You won't be able to stay. Only God can bear the weight of your devotion. Be sure there's enough of God in the thing to which you give your life, and you'll be fine.

SATURDAY IN EPIPHANY V

Pss 87, 90 * 136
Isaiah 61:10–62:5
2 Timothy 4:1–8
Mark 10:46–52

For as the earth brings forth its shoots, and as a garden causes what is sown in it to spring up . . .
ISAIAH 61:11

I like it. This is New York: There will be a group formed to oppose it by this afternoon, but I like the design that has been chosen for the World Trade Center Memorial. Just reading about it took me there.

It will be beautiful. It will be empty and full at the same time. There will be two pools of water on the location of the buildings' footprints. You'll be able to stand and stare into their depths. There will be names—ribbons of names, the designer says. Listed randomly, but there will be a directory so you can find your own person. People. There will be a row of pine trees on the outer edge of the memorial.

The familiar lurch in my stomach that I always experience whenever I think about the bombing tells me they're onto something. Pools of water to stare into. Ribbons of names. Rows of pines. Remember the ribbons of aluminum that were everywhere, peeled right off the buildings like the skin of an orange, how they festooned the site, hung on trees, lay in the street, how one of them stuck in the side of another building like an arrow that had been shot there on purpose. Remember somebody's coffee cup still visible on a desk still upright. Remember the corporate reports in folders lying on the ground, the *While You Were Out* messages on the ground like snow, how much paper survived when so many people did not, how odd that seemed. I could stare into a deep pool of water at that site for a few minutes. Or a year, maybe. I don't know for how long, but I would like the chance to stare into those pools.

Not all prayer has words. Some of the most profound prayer does not need them. They get in the way sometimes. Some prayer just stares into the middle distance, or closes its eyes and sees nothing, or gazes into a pool of water. You can stay there for as long as you wish. For as long as you need to. And then lift your eyes. There is a row of trees. Evergreens. *Oh*, you say, *I see. This is a garden now. Things grow here.*

You have to leave now. But you can come back another time.

SUNDAY, EPIPHANY VI

Pss 66, 67 * 19, 46
Isaiah 62:6–12
1 John 2:3–11
John 8:12–19

Upon your walls, O Jerusalem, I have posted sentinels . . .
ISAIAH 62:6

*W*hy are you asking me the same questions the other lady asked? Q inquires of the nurse. My heart sinks. *Why don't you be quiet?* I ask him, but I don't say it out loud.

It seems like a needless duplication of effort, he goes on. This, from a man who will drive a letter to the post office an hour before the mailman comes. He wants to be sure it gets out today.

Good Lord.

The nurse inserts an IV line and the doctor shows up to say hello. Then Q subsides into the newspaper. *Maureen Dowd is back,* he says happily. *And don't miss Friedman.*

His public-spirited daily attention to the news. His quirky humor. His household economies. His delight in the cats, his fictions about their lives. Today's procedure is not risky, but Q is in a hospital, and I can't completely relax until he is finished and home again.

Do you have any allergies? another nurse asks him, and I brace myself for his protest. But it doesn't come. Q must have absorbed something sobering. Be careful. Ask. Ask again. Assume nothing. Pay attention.

You're so bossy, he complains. It's true: I want to run everything about his hospital stay. I answer questions from medical professionals before he can open his mouth. I give him advice he did not solicit. He doesn't like it. *It's infantalizing*, he says. *Tough*, I say silently.

Love is anxious. It fears the loss of its object. To love is to know the fear of loss, and then it is to lose. *So why worry*, Q wants to know, *if there's nothing I can do about it anyway*. Rational and true, but I am built differently.

My trust in God is absolute. I know that all will be well. What it means for all to be well, though, is pretty broad, and includes all of our deaths in the arc of its graciousness.

Oh well, then. Let me worry away. Let me connect myself to him in the minutiae of medical details, and in a hundred other ways, while we are still here.

MONDAY IN EPIPHANY VI

Pss 89:1–18 * 89:19–52
Isaiah 63:1–6
1 Timothy 1:1–17
Mark 11:1–11

This saying is sure and worthy of full acceptance, that Christ Jesus came into the world to save sinners—of whom I am the foremost.
1 TIMOTHY 1:15

Next to Q's hospital bed, I find myself breaking one of the most important rules of caring for someone who is ill: I picked an argument with the patient. It was about something in the kitchen. We were miles from the kitchen. Nothing he had said was calculated to annoy me, but I took vehement exception to everything.

I'm sorry I was so mean, I said as soon as I returned to my senses.
You were . . . dramatic, he said.

I'm an actor. But I think I picked a fight because I was afraid of being afraid for him. It would be easier to see him wheeled away from me and through the double doors to the operating suite if I were angry at him. I almost knew this when I did it.

Q wouldn't fight, of course. He was calm and patient. I hate that.

As soon as you know you've crossed the line, stop and say you're sorry. Say it even if it's only half true, even if half of you is itching for the fight to go on, for just one more zinger, and leave it to your better angel to supply the other half. *Christ Jesus came into the world to save sinners*, you can say. *Of which I am one. In case you hadn't noticed.*

Do it. You don't know for sure you'll have another chance to straighten things out.

TUESDAY IN EPIPHANY VI

Pss 97, 99, (100) * 94, (95)
Isaiah 63:7–14
1 Timothy 1:18–2:8
Mark 11:12–26

He said to it, "May no one ever eat fruit from you again."
MARK 11:14

Even Jesus is having a bad behavior day: He goes to a fig tree, at a time when figs are not in season, and, finding no figs, curses it. It withers to the ground in a single day. This is the only such story about Jesus retained in the canon of scripture that eventually became the New Testament. There were more such grim stories circulated about him in the early days, but this one is the only one remaining in which we see him cursing something. Not exactly the sweet Jesus we're used to; you don't want to get on his bad side.

Hungry, tired and angry—he was truly human, we tell ourselves each time we recite one of the creeds, and that day he acted like we act. If there had been a wall nearby, he might have put his fist through it. If he had had a wife, he might have yelled at her. Might he have done worse? We do, sometimes. But Jesus? These are terrible thoughts.

Maybe the story isn't true—a story told around ancient campfires to others, not to us. Maybe we can safely discard it.

Or maybe we can think of something else, something that we don't like to think of: that Jesus' being truly human meant that he wasn't perfect, as we always say he was. That he learned like we learn—by making mistakes. That he wasn't born knowing everything. He learned and puzzled, was instructed by his parents. That his divinity, present from the first, dawned upon him and grew in his awareness, bursting forth in all its blinding force at the moment of resurrection. Intertwined, until then, with someone who was much more like us than we like to think. Because if he was more like us than we think, we could be more like him than we are.

WEDNESDAY IN EPIPHANY VI

Pss 101, 109:1–4 (5–19) 20–30 * 119:121–144
Isaiah 63:15–64:9
1 Timothy 3:1–16
Mark 11:27–12:12

The stone that the builders rejected has become the cornerstone;
this was the Lord's doing, and it is amazing in our eyes.
MARK 12:10–11

*D*amn. I had just spilled half a bag of bone meal on the front seat of the car. It had remained safely vertical on the ride to my daughter's house, where I had gone to put in a few dozen daffodils, and then it toppled over when I came up my own driveway. Most accidents happen close to home.

"I just spilled bone meal on the front seat," I announced to Q when I came in the house. "I'm sorry. I'll clean it up in the morning." But in the morning I discovered that my cool little vacuum cleaner that you charge up like a cell phone hadn't been charged up like a cell phone. I put its nose into a pile of bone meal and pulled the trigger. Nothing. It sat there like a statue of a vacuum cleaner. So the next day I used the same outlet in the bathroom we use for the sonic toothbrush and the thing charged up. It chowed down happily on the bone meal.

"I'll need to vacuum the car with the regular vacuum cleaner," Q said. "There's still some bone meal. And a little manure spilled in the trunk." I had visited the horse farm on my way back from Pennsylvania and gotten three glorious bags. "That little one doesn't pick up the heavy stuff."

Okay. But I'm going to race him and get out there first. I don't want him to vacuum up bone meal and manure that I spilled. People should handle their own . . . um, stuff.

The daffodils will be gorgeous—little stands of them here and there, deep gold and pale yellow, so pale it is almost white. Tiny ones and large trumpet ones. And the tulips will be fine, too, drifts of different colors, one shade leading into another. The bone meal undergirds it all. The manure tops it off. Gorgeous. But it's a mess getting it all there. Spilled bone meal. Manure in the trunk. Who's going to clean this up?

Horses smell wonderful. Horse manure smells wonderful. It smells of grass and grain and straw, of the chemical breaking down of everything. It is rich and alive, a dark smell, dark and warm. You get used to it. You grow into it. You understand its fecundity and admire it. Naturally, all this talk of bone meal and horse manure reminds me of the church. Look at how hard it can be to cooperate with God in the making of something beautiful. Look what a mess it can make. Look at how death enters into the process of life again, nourishing the next generation. And at how something many think unclean can feed a field of flowers.

THURSDAY IN EPIPHANY VI

Pss 105:1–22 * 105:23–45
Isaiah 65:1–12
1 Timothy 4:1–16
Mark 12:13–27

"Is it lawful to pay taxes to the emperor, or not?"
MARK 12:14

Cut taxes, we say. We say it's because government wastes money. We say it's because we're all supposed to be self-sufficient. We say a lot of things.

But we don't always like it when economic outsiders speak their truth. We want to help, of course, but feel that it really ought to be on our terms. We don't always want them to ask for what they need. Why can't they just let us tell them? Clearly, we're the ones who know how the world works. I mean, if they knew, they wouldn't be economic outsiders, now would they?

The sick and the poor, the weak, the outcast—they should try to be quiet. *We'll get to them.* We have so much to offer them, if they'll just be patient.

Sometimes we want the weak to stay weak, so that we can feel strong. We need their weakness in order to hide from our own. And sometimes we need their weakness to keep ourselves strong: Some of our power is based on the ongoing weakness of others and depends upon it. And some of our wealth depends on the poverty of others. Sometimes we fight against the very emancipation we profess to advocate. And we are annoyed when others point this out to us.

A rule of thumb: If you experience a tangible benefit from an opinion you hold, suspect yourself. If there's money in it for you, you may be a good person, but you're not a disinterested one. It's easy to believe in a tax cut if it means you'll have more money in your own pocket. It was easy to believe in slavery when a whole economy depended on it.

Remaining in that state of unconscious privilege depends on not listening to the weak. On stopping your ears against them, on closing your eyes. On not walking where they walk. Not talking to them directly, but talking above their heads, as if they could not hear. On becoming blind and deaf. Lame. Mute. More in need than you know.

FRIDAY IN EPIPHANY VI

Psalm 102 * 107:1–32
Isaiah 65:17–25
1 Timothy 5:17–22 (23–25)
Mark 12:28–34

No longer drink only water, but take a little wine for the
sake of your stomach and your frequent ailments.
1 TIMOTHY 5:23

I am embarrassed to admit that I no longer drink wine. Why embarrassed? Because I determined that I was drinking too much of it, and I lack the adult sense of moderation to drink it normally— that's the embarrassment part. A glass a day is good for the heart, you read in health magazines. *A glass a day*. That sounds good. *I can do that.*

But the fact is, I didn't do that. I had two glasses. Sometimes even three. I would station myself near the wine at dinner, to be sure of keeping my glass filled: Now, *that's* embarrassing. None of the health magazines said that three glasses of wine was good for my heart. Reluctantly, I faced facts: I can't be moderate, so I must be abstinent.

I thought it would be harder than it is. I loved wine, and Q is a wine expert: He buys the good stuff. I thought I'd feel left out, feel like a kid when everybody else was a grownup. I thought I wouldn't have any fun or be any fun. But it is not hard. I still have fun. He fixes himself one of his obscure Italian *aperitivos* and me a glass of seltzer with lemon, or a cocktail of orange juice and soda. I pour a quart of water into a little old pitcher that I love and place it on the table; by the time dinner is over, I've drunk most of it. I never have to struggle to get in all the glasses of water I know I'm supposed to be drinking. It happens naturally, during the course of the day. It's easy and sweet.

Wine is a gift from God. It says so in scripture, in several places. But not all of us can have all of God's gifts—some are for some of us and others are for others. Me, I have the gift of water, I guess.

Does it make you feel a little odd to read this? Does it even make you feel a little angry, as if I were judging your consumption of alcohol? I'm not. But if it makes you feel uncomfortable, do yourself and your health the honor of taking a look at that discomfort. Maybe there's an embarrassment ahead for you, one like mine, but I'd rather have you briefly embarrassed than ill. If there is embarrassment ahead, don't be afraid. We don't die of embarrassment, no matter what we tell each other.

SATURDAY IN EPIPHANY VI

Pss 107:33–43, 108:1–6 (7–13) * 33
Isaiah 66:1–6
1 Timothy 6:6–21
Mark 12:35–44

"For all of them have contributed out of their abundance; but she out of her poverty has put in everything she had, all she had to live on."

MARK 12:44

A lady came by, in need of money, one of a thousand such ladies who have crossed my path in the city churches I have served over the years. I was busy with something, the importance of which I cannot now remember. Funny: I don't remember my important task, but I do remember the lady.

She began to tell me where her money went: her rent, her children, the grandchildren who lived with her because their mother was strung out on drugs. She was on welfare—$565.00 was what she got every month, plus food stamps and some help with her rent. I only half listened to her recitation of her obligations, until she got to Reverend Ike.

Reverend Ike? You give money to *Reverend Ike*? I asked her—but I asked her only in my mind.

I would never miss giving to Reverend Ike, she went on, oblivious to my unvoiced objection. *I do that first, before I do anything else. Twenty dollars, every month. I never miss.*

Reverend Ike is a Harlem preacher whose gospel message is that faith in God is going to make you rich. And indeed, his life has demonstrated the truth of his gospel: His faith in God has made him very rich.

And here was this impoverished woman. A widow, giving her widow's mite, to a man with sixteen Rolls Royces.

I sat with my checkbook and thought. Thought of her need. Of her never having had enough money in her entire life, of her dream of having enough money, more than enough money, of the way Reverend Ike plays on her dream and the dreams of thousands like her every day. Some of what I was going to give her was going to go toward another diamond ring for Reverend Ike.

She took the money gratefully and put it in her worn black pocketbook. She thanked me and blessed me. *Take care of yourself first*, I told her, *before you take care of Reverend Ike. He wouldn't want you to deprive yourself and your children.* Yes, he would, I told myself angrily. He doesn't give a damn about her and her children.

She nodded politely. But as she left, I could tell that she knew I didn't really understand.

SUNDAY, EPIPHANY VII

Pss 118 * 145
Isaiah 66:7–14
1 John 3:4–10
John 10:7–16

*Before she was in labor she gave birth; before her pain came
upon her she delivered a son. Who has heard of such a thing?*

ISAIAH 66:7–8

*A*re you pregnant? I ask my visitor. He smiles, only a little surprised by the question, because he knows exactly what I mean.
Is there something new coming in your life? Do you sense a new
direction for yourself? *Are you pregnant?*

The Hebrew scriptures compare Israel to a woman so often—a
woman looking for her lover, a woman getting married, a woman
giving birth. It was a patriarchal age, we say, and it certainly was.
But ancient women live, come alive again as we read, in the imagery
of how it is with God and the people of God.

These people saw pregnancy and childbirth up close. They saw
these things as children—children of both genders stayed with the
women in ancient homes, and they saw everything. They lived with
animals and saw their birthing as well. The coyness with which we
view reproduction came much later; these people all knew.

They knew that childbirth requires patience. That it can take a
long time. That it has a progression and an order, and that bad
things can happen if the order isn't respected. The kind of birth
we know as Caesarian—because tradition has it that Julius Caesar
was born in this manner—was not part of their experience. What
they knew was a long event that was a lot of work, crowned with
joy and abundance: the ability of a woman to feed her child, even
when she is still shaking with fatigue from the effort she has
expended in her labor.

It is true that they imaged God as male, frequently. Not always,
but usually. But they imaged Israel as female much more often

than as male—the relationship between God and Israel felt to them like that between a powerful husband and a beloved wife. And they respected the power of women because they had seen it. God lives with us and empowers us to become fully what we are, they knew. Loves us. *Marries* us. And we are fruitful in that love: It causes us to birth things, to nourish and nurture things, to become strong and complete.

How do we know we're complete? That we're where we should be? We know because we are producing something, nurturing something. Pregnant with something or just delivered something—males as well as females. Something is growing because we're here. That's how we know.

MONDAY IN EPIPHANY VII

Pss 106:1–18 * 106:19–48
Ruth 1:1–14
2 Corinthians 1:1–11
Matthew 5:1–12

Then she kissed them, and they wept aloud. They said to her, "No, we will return with you to your people."
RUTH 1:9–10

Across the divide of culture and clan, the two Moabite women love their mother-in-law. No jokes about mothers-in-law are to be found in this book nor, indeed, in the rest of scripture; the relationship is not the troubled one it is so often cartooned as in our day.

Certainly they've been through enough together, the three of them. The death of all the men in the world who could protect them—nobody is left to take care of them. Disappointed hopes for children, it seems, as well—neither of the two younger women appears to be a mother. This is dangerous: Nobody has a stake in their survival. In the ancient world, as in many countries today, that's not good.

Ruth's is the kind of story we like best: The weak one comes out on top, aided by the cleverness of an older friend. A fairy godmother, or a kindly witch. Here, a mother-in-law. Naomi will take a deep breath and look around to see what can be done. And she will notice that Ruth, the daughter-in-law who stays with her, is still very pretty. And off we go.

I wonder what happened to Orpah, the one who obeyed her mother-in-law and left? She went back home to her own people. I wonder if anyone there took care of her, if there was a smart older woman at home who could help her come out on top, too? We have no way of knowing. We never hear of Orpah again.

The story makes me think that we're better off facing into our futures, even if they're full of unknown quantities. There's nothing back home for us now. We're not from there any more.

TUESDAY IN EPIPHANY VII

Pss (120), 121, 122, 123 * 124, 125, 126, (127)
Ruth 1:15–22
2 Corinthians 1:12–22
Matthew 5:13–20

*"You are the salt of the earth; but if salt has lost
its taste, how shall its saltiness be restored?"*

MATTHEW 5:13

Now, salt doesn't *lose* its taste: It's a mineral, not an herb, and it retains its saltiness. Come back a thousand years later and lick a salt block: It will still be salty. Salt is like a rock. So what does Jesus mean? He means it doesn't happen. Any more than people light a lamp and then hide the light. That doesn't happen either.

People alive with faith show it. They change things around them. They make the bland salty, the dark light. Nothing is the same as it was before they came around. They retain their peculiarity. They keep their strength. And they influence their surroundings with it.

We don't have religious conversions for the short term. God doesn't come and spend the weekend with us and then go away. We may be ephemeral, but God is not, and neither is faith. Faith moves in and stays. If yours didn't, it wasn't faith. Try again.

That is not to say that faith feels the same all the time. It lives with the other parts of your life, seasoning everything in you. It blends with whatever else comprises you. It intensifies the richness you already have. You have the same history you always had, but faith causes you to view it in a different light—now it seems that certain things were purposeful, *meant to be*, you sometimes think to yourself. *This had to happen*, you think as you remember. Faith organizes your history differently in your memory. *Now I get it*, you think.

My life, like everyone else's, contains happy and sad days. Good and bad things have happened to me, and I have also done good and bad things. Not all the bad things I have done were finished by the time I became a person of faith, either. I don't ever remember not being a person of faith, and I've been a mixed bag all along.

But you could always taste the salt.

WEDNESDAY IN EPIPHANY VII

Pss 119:145–176 *128, 129, 130
Ruth 2:1–13
2 Corinthians 1:23–2:17
Matthew 5:21–26

". . . first be reconciled to your brother or sister,
and then come and offer your gift."
MATTHEW 5:24

The Peace was not, shall we say, *universally popular* when it came out in the 1960s. *Why are we doing this?* people wondered. *Why must we run around the church and clap each other on the back, as if it were a Rotary Club meeting?* It was jarring, that jocular moment in the midst of a worship service. Some people have never gotten over their discomfort and at their most effusive can muster only a cool nod and a two-fingered handshake. It'll just have to do.

Others are like Golden Retrievers, bounding among the pews, squealing greetings at each other like long-lost relatives, standing around in groups of three or four and catching up on each others' weeks. It can take ten minutes to restore order. Many people are very proud of this, pointing out how long the Peace takes at their church as if it were a badge of honor. *This is how friendly a place we are,* the Peace marathon says. *This is how much we love each other.*

The Peace, though, was never intended to be a social occasion. That's why God made Coffee Hour. The Peace is about something else: It is specifically about reconciliation between Christians who have quarreled. And it is on the basis of this verse from Matthew. The sacrament of unity among Christians would not be celebrated against a backdrop of ongoing enmity. If you were estranged from someone, you sought him out and reconciled. Only after you had done so could you present yourself at the table to receive the Body and Blood of Christ.

At the peace, go first to the person in the congregation with whom you have the most difficulty. You needn't fling yourself into her arms. A warm handshake or a brief hug is just fine. Things need not be completely *settled* between you, either—that will probably take some work. But the Peace is a sign of readiness to relate as sisters and brothers in Christ, no matter what has gone before.

THURSDAY IN EPIPHANY VII

Pss 131, 132, (133) * 134, 135
Ruth 2:14–23
2 Corinthians 3:1–18
Matthew 5:27–37

"It is better, my daughter, that you go out with his young women, otherwise you might be bothered in another field."
RUTH 2:22

A perennial fear throughout the world: that a woman's physical weakness in comparison with that of a man might put her in danger. That she might be raped if she strays too far from the company of someone who can keep her safe.

In this scene, we notice also that this fear arises from her economic and social inferiority, not just her lack of physical strength. Ruth has no power. No place. No status. She needs protection.

Boaz has a small group of young women who live and work under his care. It is likely that he will have sexual relations with some or all of them—that was probably part of the arrangement. Ruth is on her way to becoming one of them.

A gritty reality, that of Ruth and Naomi and Boaz. Not a way we would want to live. But many people in the world still live this way today. As hard a way of life as it is, Naomi and Ruth clearly find it preferable to many other things that could be happening. This may not be the way we would like it to be, but it sure could be worse.

When we read of such things in scripture, does it mean that God favors arrangements like this? Is everything in the Bible the way things should be? Many people want that to be the case, want there to be a biblical standard of marriage and relationship between the sexes to which we can all aspire and within which we can all live. But stories like this one show us that this certainty cannot be ours. History has moved from the time of Ruth and Naomi, at least in more privileged parts of the world. Women no longer have to place themselves under the protection of a man in order to retain their physical safety—at least, they don't have to do that here. Many things have changed, and we have had to change with them.

FRIDAY IN EPIPHANY VII

Pss 140, 142 * 141, 143:1–11 (12)
Ruth 3:1–18
2 Corinthians 4:1–12
Matthew 5:38–48

*"My daughter, I need to seek some security
for you, so that it may be well with you."*
RUTH 3:1

My son's girlfriend came by today, my visitor says. Her face is sad. *Ah,* I say. Ordinarily that would not be news, but it is: Her son has been dead for five years.

She brought her fiance with her, she goes on. *She wanted me to meet him.*

Oh, I say.

It's hard to know how to respond. Nobody would desire a young woman to put her life on hold forever because of a tragedy in her youth. And yet what mother would not meet the prospective husband of her dead son's beloved and wish that the two men could change places?

And here is Naomi, so busy matchmaking on behalf of the widow of her dead son. Pushing thoughts of her boy out of her mind, I suppose, in order to concentrate on the delicate maneuvers she must perform, even setting up a sexual encounter between Ruth and Boaz to attract his interest—the word rendered in most Bibles as "feet" is actually the Hebrew word for "genitals." That is the part of Boaz that Ruth uncovered on the threshing floor. In asking him to "spread his skirt" over her, she is requesting that he perform the duty of a male relative toward her deceased husband: marry his widow.

Life must go on. That is what this ancient custom was all about: The children born of a union between Boaz and Ruth would be children born on behalf of the dead husband. Even the dead were entitled to the fruits of their lives, to children who would remember whose they were.

Can we see beyond the strangeness of this ancient practice to our own longing? Can our lives go on, too, even after we have lost someone we loved more than life itself? Can we find the courage Naomi found within herself to create a means of remembering her son? Can we help to make the world a better place because they were here, even if they are here no longer?

When we no longer have the things on which we depend, we learn to depend on other things. We use what we have. Human beings are resourceful. And human life goes on.

SATURDAY IN EPIPHANY VII

Pss 137:1–6 (7–9), 144 * 104
Ruth 4:1–17
2 Corinthians 4:13–5:10
Matthew 6:1–6

"So we are always confident . . ."
2 CORINTHIANS 5:6

Rain, again. But it is nice and warm here on the train, and the convent will be nice and warm, too, when I get there, just a few puddles away from the subway stop.

Anna is inside at her restaurant. It should be nice and warm in there, too.

Corinna is inside at her school, and Rosie and Madeline are inside at their respective schools. Nice and warm.

All the cats are in. Kate hid from us this morning because she heard us talking about taking her to the vet. She came out after I called the vet to cancel. We still don't know where she was all that time. Remind me not to talk about the vet in front of Kate.

But Q is out. He doesn't care about the weather and never has. Doesn't talk about it much, like other people do. In the heat of summer or in a blizzard, he likes to be outside. Hopping over my New York city puddles, I daydream of Q in his chair in the lamplight, reading a book, with Kate in my chair watching him read, which she can do for hours without ever getting bored. But that's a daydream. He is likely to be outside somewhere.

The ancients were much less insulated from the weather than we are. More like Q, I guess. Q must be an ancient. But they talk about the weather more than he does and use it to describe the awesome power of God. Or, as Jesus does here, the daunting forces that confront us as we try to live our lives. Get inside, he says. Think about the future and provide for it. Build a strong house that will keep you safe. During a rainstorm is a poor time to begin. Do it now, before the weather turns.

SUNDAY, EPIPHANY VIII

Pss 146, 147 * 111, 112, 113
Deuteronomy 4:1–9
2 Timothy 4:1–8
John 12:1–8

And what other great nation has statutes and ordinances as just as this entire law that I am setting before you today?
DEUTERONOMY 4:8

You know that in the time of Jesus, as had been the case for centuries before him, the worship in the Temple at Jerusalem was animal sacrifice. Rich people brought perfect lambs there to sacrifice, while poor people brought birds because they were cheaper—Mary and Joseph brought a pair of doves, remember? You could buy the animals in the front of the temple—that's what all the money changers were doing there that day when Jesus overturned their tables. They were supposed to be there, changing secular money into the special temple coin used to buy special animals.

The throats of the animals were slit and their blood poured out. Their flesh was burned and the priests got to take some home. It must have smelled, literally, to high heaven. That's what worship was like in the Temple. So when the Temple was destroyed, it was this worship, the cult of animal sacrifice, that would henceforth be denied the people of Israel.

They experienced this as the worst thing that could have happened to them. To this day, Jews pray for its restoration.

But it was this tragedy that set them free. No more animal sacrifice. They left Jerusalem, scattered all over the world, taking with them the only thing that could have survived the centuries. Not animal sacrifice. Not worship tied to a specific temple in a specific city. They could only take what they could carry with them.

They took the majesty of their ethical heritage. The holiness of the Law. Henceforth, they would be known as the people whose God was characterized by righteousness, who valued righteousness in his people more than he valued any cultic sacrifice they could make. It would be goodness, not sacrifice, that made a Jew good. That was what they had, all they had left. And it would be all they needed.

MONDAY IN EPIPHANY VIII

Pss 1, 2, 3 * 4, 7
Deuteronomy 4:9–14
2 Corinthians 10:1–18
Matthew 6:7–15

*"When you are praying, do not heap up empty
phrases as the Gentiles do; for they think that they
will be heard because of their many words."*
MATTHEW 6:7

I just don't know whether to pray that she get well or not, someone
says in a troubled whisper, leaving a hospital room—*she's so sick.*
As if the words we use in prayer will determine the outcome of a
person's illness: Say the right words and she gets better. Get it wrong
and she's gone.

Of course we don't think that. But it does suggest something to
me about words in prayer: Most of us use way too many of them.
We get carried away with our own interior voices, and then we can't
take time to listen for God's voice. Our own is sounding in our ears
all the time. And sometimes our words and our anxiety about them
get seriously in our way, highjack us into dead ends of anger or fear,
dead ends that obscure our vision of God and impair our trust.
What if . . . ? How could he . . . ? Why can't I . . . ? We can chase our
own tails with words like these for a long time.

Actually, it's not necessary to say anything in prayer at all. Ever.
About anything. We need only fall silent and rest in the presence of
God. God already knows who we are, what's going on inside us, what
we need, what we fear. We can talk to God if we want to, but never
think that using the wrong words with God will get you into trouble.

Sometimes, though, you just need a little something in the way
of a word or two to get started. The prayer Jesus suggests is as good
as any. In the contemporary version, it's fifty-six words long. And
there's really nothing missing.

TUESDAY IN EPIPHANY VIII

Pss 5, 6 * 10, 11
Deuteronomy 4:15–24
2 Corinthians 11:1–21a
Matthew 6:16–23

". . . and your Father who sees in secret will reward you."
MATTHEW 6:18

St. Paul's Chapel in New York City, famous nationwide during the aftermath of the World Trade Center bombing as a respite center for rescue workers, was famous before that, of course. It is the oldest continuously used building in Manhattan, and it is a treasure of eighteenth-century American architecture.

It was the great and near-great of New York who built St. Paul's. You see their names on the walls, engraved on elegant marble and granite tablets, remembering this wealthy woman, that wealthy man. A soldier fallen in battle. A young man lost at sea. Wealthy yellow fever victims from the city's epidemic early in the nineteenth century.

And one philanthropist whose mourners chose this verse with which to honor him, with one important difference. Here is how his memorial tablet reads:

And your Father who sees in secret will reward you openly.

"Openly?" Wait a minute. There's no "openly" in the Biblical text.

I guess those very public and practical people couldn't bear the thought that some good deeds might be completely unsung. That virtue really might have to be its own reward sometimes, all by itself. That it's not a sure thing that doing good does us good in this life.

The life of their friends might have instructed them in this—by all indications, a good and generous man, but he was cut down in the prime of life by the fever that swept the malarial swamps of Lower Manhattan. As dead as the biggest scoundrel in his neighborhood, once the wrong bug got hold of him.

I will never visit St. Paul's again without thinking of how it was after 9/11. Of all the people who struggled there to find someone alive, and then just to find someone. Of how devoted they were and how sad. I hardly know any of their names. Some of them were paid, but most of them were volunteers. I don't think they gave a thought to getting a reward. Finding someone alive would have been all the reward they would ever have needed. Most of them didn't get that.

But their Father who sees in secret will reward them.

WEDNESDAY IN EPIPHANY VIII

Pss 119:1–24 * 12, 13, 14
Deuteronomy 4:25–31
2 Corinthians 11:21b–33
Matthew 6:24–34

*"Consider the lilies of the field, how they
grow; they neither toil nor spin . . ."*
MATTHEW 6:28

It's been in the high thirties and even in the forties for a few days now. *Let me go see if the crocuses are up,* I think during a lull in my creativity. And they are: tiny spikes of dark green stem scattered across the brown soil at the base of the big tree out back, more along the driveway, a few more in the little bed outside the back door.

Oh, good.

Even if the groundhog was right (he always predicts six more weeks of winter, hasn't predicted anything else since I've been alive, so I don't know why they even bother asking him), it won't be long now. Spring is coming. The air is softening. The days are longer. Even if it does snow again, it can't snow too many more times.

I guess I will never get so old that my heart does not leap when I see the first shoots of spring. I guess I'll thrill to them for as long as I can walk out there and see them. I'll bet anything I will thrill to them if I have to be wheeled outside in a chair to take a look, and I hope there is somebody who can take the time to help me get outside.

The closer I get to death, the more comfort I take in the ongoingness of the world. That the flowers will still grow, that birds will still sing. I will be gone, but nature will still be here.

And not only will it still be here, I will be a part of it. My molecules will get a new lease on life; once their work on my behalf is finished, they will turn to other pursuits: nourishing plants and earthworms, at first, and then becoming part of another animal who is not me. And they're off and running again.

Meanwhile, I will be focused on other things. I will finally know what heaven is, finally know what it is to be undivided in my heart. I will know things I do not now know.

And, back on the earth, the flowers will still grow.

THURSDAY IN EPIPHANY VIII

Pss 18:1–20 * 18:21–50
Deuteronomy 4:32–40
2 Corinthians 12:1–10
Matthew 7:1–12

*"Ask, and it will be given you; search, and you will
find; knock, and the door will be opened for you."*
MATTHEW 7:7

My 1:00 P.M. appointment has yet to appear, and it is now 1:30. How rude. But also, how delightful—the God of Cancellation has smiled on me unexpectedly, and I have some bonus time.

Any schedule south of that administered by the Secret Service must have some give in it, and even the Secret Service has a Plan B. Things happen that are outside of my control. I have a choice about how I will greet those things. I can allow myself to be unnerved by them, or I can assume that there is a hidden delight somewhere among their wreckage.

Today, for instance, I am in the desperate throes of an impending deadline. I need to center my thoughts, and I need to write. I need to write *a lot*. I now have an hour in which to write, an hour I didn't think I would have. I am that much closer to my deadline. I just may get there.

I think there's a gift in every setback. Everything that doesn't work out leaves space for something else that can. That possibility is part of what God is, I think, spinning new possibilities for us right on the spot, using the very debris of our broken hopes as the raw material of the new thing.

God is the Creator. We think of the creation as something that happened a long time ago, billions of years, maybe. But the Creator is at work now—each of us is a creation, and each tree, each animal, each mountain. It's ongoing, not just an event in the past.

And it happens out of the rubble of defeat. God uses things that don't work to make things that do. Our false starts are the beginnings of our thankful AMENs at the end of something wonderful. We can trust this process—creating is what the Creator does. Not just a long time ago. Right now, on the spot. Ask. Seek. Knock. If it doesn't exist yet, God will make it. And you, perhaps, will help.

FRIDAY IN EPIPHANY VIII

Pss 16, 17 * 22
Deuteronomy 5:1–22
2 Corinthians 12:11–21
Matthew 7:13–21

For I am not at all inferior to these
super-apostles, even though I am nothing.
2 CORINTHAINS 12:11

Hee hee. Listen to Paul, easily the most sarcastic person in the Bible. Today he's peeved because the Corinthians don't seem to be according him the proper respect. Both letters to the Corinthians drip with sarcasm—watch out for compliments in the Corinthian letters. Hint: None of them are sincere.

But behind the biting remarks—sarcasm means, literally, "to tear the flesh"—I hear hurt feelings. We know that there was something about Paul that might have made people laugh at him: the "thorn in the flesh" he mentioned in yesterday's lesson. Some affliction that embarrassed him—did he stammer, maybe, or might he have had a seizure disorder? Whatever it was, it seems that Paul struggled again and again to be taken seriously, to be heard and valued. People who sense a deficit in self-worth are often defensive. Strike first, before someone strikes you. Get them before they get you. They take things personally. Paul sure does—*If I loved you more, am I to be loved less?*

Think of it: One of the most important people in the early church might well have been a disabled person. The one whose preaching ensured that people outside the community of first-century Israel heard the gospel may have been disabled. Until rather recently, people with disabilities ordinarily could not be ordained to the priesthood. If Paul really *was* disabled, that doesn't make a whole lot of sense. In fact, it makes little sense even if he wasn't. The gifts of the spirit that a leader wants to encourage aren't primarily the physical ones. We can condition our bodies on our own: All we have to do is work at it. And if they can't do every blessed thing we might like them to do, it doesn't slow the spirit down in the least.

And not only disabled—cranky! If you haven't gotten over your youthful illusion that the saints were all sweetness and light, Paul should fix you right up. If he doesn't, and you really want to scare yourself, read Jerome.

Cranky people. People who don't do everything perfectly. People who have known hurt in life. God calls us all. I feel better already.

SATURDAY IN EPIPHANY VIII

Pss 20, 21:1–7 (8–14) * 110:1-5 (6–7), 116, 117
Deuteronomy 5:22–33
2 Corinthians 13:1–14
Matthew 7:22–29

"I never knew you; go away from me, you evildoers."
MATTHEW 7:23

The New Testament contains many descriptions of the last judgment like this one: Be on the right side, they all say, or at the end of time Jesus will not choose you. It will be like those terrible, unforgettable moments in elementary school then, when you were last to be chosen to be on a team. So that's what it'll be like, then: It's a competition in the afterlife, just as it is here on the earth.

We were hoping for something different.

And I think what we have is something different. That the people writing the many different books and letters that comprise these earliest documents of our faith were preoccupied with the end of the world is clear. They thought it was imminent, a matter of months, a year or two at the most. Then the time got longer as the years went by. *Maybe it's going to be a thousand years.* We see them getting discouraged, see them begin to allegorize things they had taken literally in the early days. *I guess Jesus isn't coming back right away, like he said. I guess it's going to be a while. I guess I don't know when. I guess we're not supposed to know.*

Maybe he's not coming. Nobody ever said that. I wonder if any of them thought it.

They wrote out of who they were. Who they were was competitive and afraid of being wrong, defensive of their territory and their ways, anxious about being overrun by other cultures. In short, they were rather like us. They imagined that God was probably like that, too: territorial, anxious, defensive. We imagine that, as well.

But God is very different from us. We don't get very far at all in our project of imagining God. Mostly, we try to stay in touch: to be still and hear the voice of God, always aware that we tend to mistake other voices for his. *I never knew you*, a gatekeeper Jesus says at the end of time, in the imagination of a New Testament writer. But he does know us. Better than we know ourselves.

SUNDAY, LAST EPIPHANY

Pss 148, 149, 150 * 114, 115
Deuteronomy 6:1–9
Hebrews 12:18–29
John 12:24–32

Hear, O Israel: The Lord is our God, the Lord alone.
You shall love the Lord your God with all your heart,
and with all your soul, and with all your might.
DEUTERONOMY 6:4–5

Of course, the sunset is not a message from God. We know that. Its glorious colors betoken nothing more than the presence of various gasses in the earth's atmosphere. That's all. We know that.

Or do we? Why, if it is just a chemical moment, is it so lovely to us? Why does it take our breath away? What happens in all of our brains to convince us that the sunset is lovely? What stops us in our tracks to gaze upon it, until the last red edge of it has vanished below the horizon? Why do we all agree about that beauty, we who agree with our fellows about so few other things?

It is hard not to ascribe creative intent to the beauties of the earth. And is it such a silly thing to do, really, to look at the creation and glimpse the Creator? Must an understanding of the slow grandeur of the earth's evolution war with a lively sense of a personal God?

The talk on the train out of Albany is of politics, as it was on the train there. Intent on their subject, nobody noticed the spectacular sunset: orange, gold, purple, silver, and blue, radiating from a gold center of light. Some pretty powerful people were on this train; I could tell from the conversation. But right outside their windows, a demonstration of much more power was winding down. Now just the faintest touch of gold at the horizon, and then it disappeared.

MONDAY IN LAST EPIPHANY

Pss 25 * 9, 15
Deuteronomy 6:10–15
Hebrews 1:1–14
John 1:1–18

When the Lord your God has brought you into the land that he swore to your ancestors, to Abraham, to Isaac, and to Jacob, to give you—a land with fine, large cities that you did not build, houses filled with all sorts of goods that you did not fill, hewn cisterns that you did not hew . . .

DEUTERONOMY 6:10–11

So there were already people in the land promised to the Hebrews. People who had lived there for centuries, in cities. For many years, the Hebrews attacked and raided those cities. The people there raided back. They killed each other back and forth for a long time before the Hebrews won and the land became Israel. The Holy Land. So the Holy Land has been bloody for a while. A long time.

But what has never been true was that there were no people there. It was never empty. When the Great Powers—notably England and the United States—talked about "a land without people for a people without a land," meaning Palestine and the Jews, it wasn't the truth. It never has been. No wonder it's so troubled there. It's never been anything else.

We need to—gently, for these ideas are old and venerated—move away from the idea that God gives some people land and takes it from other people. People take land from each other, and they use talk about God as a cover for their aggression. The earth belongs to God, not to any people. Nobody owns land. We keep it in trust from

God. Nobody has a right to it. God give us a season on the earth as a gift and a sacred trust. Not as a right.

Remember the Lord, this passage says, when you come into this promised land. Remember the righteousness God requires. Learn and grow in that righteousness. And maybe someday you will have grown enough to honor the image of God in all people, not only in your own countrymen.

TUESDAY IN LAST EPIPHANY

Pss 26, 28 * 36, 39
Deuteronomy 6:16–25
Hebrews 2:1–10
John 1:19–28

. . . Then you shall say to your children, "We were Pharoah's slaves in Egypt, but the Lord brought us out of Egypt with a mighty hand."
DEUTERONOMY 6:21

Not much is said about how the Hebrews became Pharoah's slaves in the first place. We can go back to Joseph and his brothers, and the relocating of all the sons of Jacob in Egypt after Joseph makes his good fortune known to his former tormentors. And then time passes and the writer informs us simply that a new pharaoh arose "who did not know Joseph." Suddenly the people are slaves. And the story of the Exodus begins.

We don't really know what happened. The day-to-day series of growing abuses that would result in this terrible state of affairs. When things first began to go wrong. We know nothing of any of this. We just know that they were slaves now and that somebody needed to help them get free.

When we're in prison—not the kind with bars of iron, but some prison of our own making—we are liable to want very much to understand how we got there. *Why did this happen? Why am I here?*

How did I get in this situation? And it would be good to know why, good to know how. Good, so that we don't go down the same road again if we ever find ourselves in a similar situation in the future.

But now, when you're *in* the prison, how and why you got there is not what you need to focus on first. What you need to know first is how you can get out. And the Exodus was that story: the story of how the children of Israel got out. That's what you're supposed to remember, what you're supposed to tell your little boy. Tell him how we got out. God brought us out. And now we belong to God, and we measure all our behavior by its fidelity to the God who helped us get free.

People in recovery from addiction all got free. They don't ask themselves much why they were addicts; that seems a pretty easy question to them. *I drank because I was a drunk*, they say in a meeting, and everyone laughs a little. But they spend the rest of their lives learning to *stay* free, learning to know themselves and their hidden agendas, their weak points, the lies they tell, and the truths they know.

Getting free is a mighty act of God. And staying free is the holy work of a human being in partnership with God.

Lent

ASH WEDNESDAY

Pss 95, 32, 143 * 102, 130
Jonah 3:1–4:11
Hebrews 12:1–14
Luke 18:9–14

"God, be merciful to me, a sinner!"
LUKE 18:13

I don't know why some people don't want to talk about sin, or why they experience the idea of sin as burdensome. I find it immensely freeing. I am a sinner: I have scores of things in my life that are not as I wish they were. Some of them are not my fault, but some of them are.

The good news is that I don't need to conceal this fact. I don't need to struggle to present myself before God or anyone else as spotless. I am far from spotless, and God knows it well. I don't have to be ashamed of my load of sin. I don't have to bear it alone.

As a matter of fact, I don't have to bear it at all. I don't have to stay right where I am, doomed to repeat the same destructive behaviors again and again, without ever learning from my mistakes. It is never too late to change, and the weight of change, while it may be too much for me to contemplate without feeling a little ill, is never too heavy for God to lift.

Don't like something in yourself? Want something to be different? Today is a good day to begin a new relationship with that old enemy. Of course, if you have lived with it for a long time, it has acquired an extensive wardrobe of fraudulent clothes, designed to make you think you can't possibly live without it. But you can.

As we have been created, we contain within ourselves all we need to be every good thing we can be. Our counter-urges, our self-destructive and other-destructive ways—these things are not integral to us. Only the good is truly us. The rest we can do without.

So today's the day, maybe. *Wash me clean, Lord. Start with me today. Be aware, as I know you are aware, that I may fight you at first, preferring the devil I know to the goodness of which I can, at present, only dream. But start now anyway, Lord. I am ready.*

THURSDAY AFTER ASH WEDNESDAY

Pss 37:1–18 * 37:19–42
Deuteronomy 7:6–11
Titus 1:1–16
John 1:29–34

It was not because you were more numerous than any other people that the Lord set his heart on you and chose you—for you were the fewest of all peoples. It was because the Lord loved you and kept the oath that he swore to your ancestors, that the Lord has brought you out with a mighty hand, and redeemed you from the house of slavery, from the hand of Pharaoh king of Egypt.

DEUTERONOMY 7:7–8

This is what we can't believe—that God's love for us is not somehow tied up with our absorption in our own power. Surely we are better than other people. Surely that is what it is to be chosen of God. Somehow, this must all be about our deserving.

But it isn't. Not our deserving, or our power, or our wit, or anything else. The brightest among us is not in a better position than the most modestly endowed where God is concerned. God is so far above us that the differences between us fade into meaninglessness before the divine power.

God doesn't love us because we're strong. It's the other way around, actually. We're strong as a result of the love of God poured out upon us. It is this love that fuels any excellence we may muster.

This is very orthodox thinking. Many people have appropriated it into their lives to their detriment, thinking that the fact that God's love doesn't arise from our worth means that we *have* no worth, that we're terrible, stained, evil. No. We're not evil. We're sort of neutral, at least we are when we arrive on the scene. Life happens all over us, though, and most of us get a little shopworn as we go along. Life saps our strength.

And so God chooses us again and again. The Exodus happened generations after the covenant with Abraham, and the coming of Christ happened generations after the Exodus. In between God sent prophet after prophet to remind the people of their chosenness. God isn't trying to make it hard for us. God isn't hiding from us. There are many chances for us to wake up to the love of God. At least one will come your way this very day.

FRIDAY AFTER ASH WEDNESDAY

Pss 95, 31 * 35
Deuteronomy 7:12–16
Titus 2:1–15
John 1:35–42

*Show yourself in all respects a model of good
works, and in your teaching show integrity, gravity,
and sound speech that cannot be censured . . .*
TITUS 2:7–8

The rain has washed away almost all of the snow, and decent-sized rivers race along the curb to the grid that covers the drain. The street lamps light the slight mist of rain still falling, soft yellow globes of light around each bright center. The headlights and taillights of cars and busses hit the wet pavement and dissolve into its depths. People walk gingerly, stepping from spot to spot of slightly higher and therefore slightly drier sidewalk, taking the long way around the lakes that have formed at each intersection. Sometimes there is no long way. Then they slosh straight through the little seas, cursing as they go.

Strip away what you know about the effect of water on fine leather, and about catching your death of cold, and you will remember that sloshing through a water puddle feels wonderful. There's not a kid alive who doesn't love to do this. By the time we're grown, though, we've let people talk us into believing it's unpleasant.

The veneer of civilization homogenizes us. Old pleasures become uncouth, and we find it difficult to admit that we ever enjoyed them. The rare person who resists this process is shunned as the dangerous person he is: What if we all just went out and walked in the puddles every time it rained? What then? Who would do all the work?

We would. We'd indulge ourselves and then we'd come back inside and return to our adult tasks. The holy secret is that we can be both the children we once were and the adults we are now, and that one need not be at the expense of the other.

SATURDAY AFTER ASH WEDNESDAY

Pss 30, 32 * 42, 43
Deuteronomy 7:17–26
Titus 3:1–15
John 1:43–51

But avoid stupid controversies, genealogies, dissensions, and quarrels about the law, for they are unprofitable and worthless.
TITUS 3:9

Two Jews, three opinions, Brad tells me. *It's an old saying. We could no more not argue than not breathe.*

It's the Jewish way to truth: discuss, argue, read, and argue some more. The argument is part of the truth. A page of Talmud is even set up like an argument—the snippet of scripture text in the middle, surrounded by commentaries on all four sides. You can literally see the rabbis argue about the text, right there on the page.

So why does Paul want people to stop arguing? And what on earth makes him think they can?

It seems that there are stupid arguments and then there are others that are not stupid.

Anyone who has been around the church for any length of time knows a stupid argument when he hears one. One person loves the sound of his own voice and just can't seem to turn it off, and another insists on cartooning his opponent. Someone else gets up and leaves.

People Regress in Churches, read a sign that used to hang in the parish office. Why do people walk in here and begin to act like cranky toddlers? Because *People Regress in Churches*. Why do they do things they wouldn't think of trying at work? *People Regress in Churches*. They may look fifty-five, but inside they're really four years old.

Now, what can you do with these large children?

I think you have to speak to the adult. Interact with the adult, encourage the adult, give your attention to the adult, and do not reward the childish behavior with any attention. Do it this way in all possible cases—an exception must be made when someone is actually going to be harmed in some way, of course, but for the most part, you can help a person behave in a way worthy of his own forgotten dignity by treating him as if he already were.

SUNDAY, LENT I

Pss 63:1–8 (9–11), 98 * 103
Deuteronomy 8:1–10
1 Corinthians 1:17–31
Mark 2:18–22

Christ did not send me to baptize but to proclaim
the gospel, and not with eloquent wisdom, so that the
cross of Christ might not be emptied of its power.
1 CORINTHIANS 1:17

A moment of embarrassment, worthy of an adolescent but odd on a fiftyish grandmother: A luncheon companion wants to know if I've read much among recent books in psychology about forgiveness. This is a reasonable question, since I travel around the country speaking about forgiveness. But no, I hadn't. He mentioned a couple of titles. No and No. Oh, dear. I hadn't done my homework.

I'm sorry, I said. *I'm not much of a researcher*. That's an understatement.

Paul, of all people, leaps to my defense. It turns out that too much learning empties the cross of its power.

Oh.

So Christ is better proclaimed by those of us who are dumber than dirt than by those with lots of Op.Cits and Ibids. I'm in.

That luncheon was almost a week ago, and I'm still embarrassed. Still worrying about whether the guy thinks I'm stupid. Or a fraud. I never claim to be an academic, but I guess I've never stopped feeling vaguely guilty for not being one. As if their work, with its yards of footnotes and miles of bibliography, were the real work, and mine were just fluff.

And maybe mine *is* just fluff. Who knows, maybe yours is, too. We may not be intellectual heavyweights. Or we may be. Or maybe we used to be, until we forgot most of what we knew. But whichever we are—academic or not, brilliant or not, wise from reading or wise from living or both—there is a gospel to be proclaimed by living it. You don't learn everything there is to know in school, but you do learn what you learn, and we do put all of what we know—wherever we learned it—in the service of being the good news for those into whose lives we find ourselves sent.

MONDAY IN LENT I

Pss 41, 52 * 44
Deuteronomy 8:11–20
Hebrews 2:11–18
John 2:1–12

*On the third day there was a wedding in Cana
of Galilee, and the mother of Jesus was there. Jesus and
his disciples had also been invited to the wedding.*

JOHN 2:1–2

There were six jars and each held twenty or thirty gallons of water. That's 120–180 gallons of wine he made that day, something like 500 modern bottles. That's a lot of wine. The only people who weren't delighted, I imagine, were the servants who had to go back to the well and fetch 180 more gallons of water for the washing up.

Weddings have to be perfect. People have to pore over catalogues to find the perfect "Bill and Suzy" matchbooks, wonder why they need "enclosure envelopes" for their invitations, feel the first stirrings of dislike begin at the mother-in-law's slowness in choosing the fabric for her dress. People who don't know much about entertaining are easy targets for people who sell weddings, and they relieve them of multiple thousands of dollars, not a dollar of which can guarantee that anything that happens on the great day will be tasteful. Looking cheap can be very expensive.

But the wedding will be beautiful: The bride will be beautiful, the mothers lovelier than they've been for years, the men unexpectedly handsome in their formal attire. The food will be great, and the wine. Anything that goes amiss will make the wedding memorable. Let's wait and see what it is.

TUESDAY IN LENT I

Pss 45 * 47, 48
Deuteronomy 9:4–12
Hebrews 3:1–11
John 2:13–22

*Making a whip of cords, he drove all of them out of the temple,
both the sheep and the cattle. He also poured out the coins
of the money changers and overturned their tables.*

JOHN 2:15

Animal sacrifice—that was the temple worship Jesus knew. Mary and Joseph brought doves to the Temple to sacrifice, as a thank-offering when he was born. They brought doves because they were poor: If they'd been wealthier, they would have brought a lamb. Every day, animals were killed there by the hundreds. The blood poured out on the altar and the flesh burned.

Should time travel ever become a reality, don't ever agree to be on the altar guild at the Temple in Jerusalem. No matter what they tell you.

So what is Jesus doing in destroying the means by which people buy animals to sacrifice? Perhaps he is preparing for a completely different view of what a relationship with God requires, preparing for the eventuality that, forty years after his crucifixion, would become a reality: The Temple was destroyed. There would be no more animal sacrifice, not ever again.

Something else would have to take its place. In Judaism, that something else already existed, had since the last dispersion under the heel of the Babylonians. It was the synagogue, an assembly for prayer and study that still exists today. It was in a synagogue in his home town, not in the Temple at Jerusalem, that Jesus proclaimed the time of fulfillment that so shocked his friends and neighborhood: *This day the scripture is fulfilled in your hearing.*

A smaller structure, but a bigger God. The synagogue could be anywhere and everywhere, just like the church would be.

Never think that things can't change. Even important things. Even things that have been around forever. And never think it's the end of the world if they do. God always has another way.

WEDNESDAY IN LENT I

Pss 119:49–72 * 49, (53)
Deuteronomy 9:13–21
Hebrews 3:12–19
John 2:23–3:15

Take care, brothers and sisters, that none of you may have an evil, unbelieving heart that turns away from the living God.
HEBREWS 3:12

So, are doubts "evil"? Because if they are, most of us are pretty bad.

I don't know a person of faith who doesn't have doubts. Sometimes they are mild, niggling puzzlements about the authority of this or that detail of scripture. And sometimes they are enormous and terrible, real crises of faith that hold before our eyes the awful possibility that we might be all alone here, that no God loves us or anybody else. That there is nothing beyond what we see.

Terrible, I say. Of course, you and I know that many of our friends and neighbors, and not a few of our family members, live with this belief every day. Many modern people don't think there's a God and seem perfectly content to have it so. On Sunday mornings, when we are at the church setting up the coffee hour or herding acolytes, they're home with the paper or hauling two different kids to two different soccer games. They don't pray and don't miss it. They're good citizens who do good things. *Terrible* is not a word one would use to describe their lives.

So the evil of an unbelieving heart is certainly not an ethical evil.

The Christians of the third and fourth centuries used to speak of evil as a "privation of the good." Existence itself was good, they said, and what we call evil is simply a hole in it, a lessening of what is. In a sense, then, it can be said that evil is, literally, non-existence. Everything that *is*, insofar as it *is*, is good. So life is good; disease is evil because it destroys life. Love is good; addiction is evil because it destroys love. Peace is good; war is evil because it destroys peace.

Not, perhaps, the most satisfying definition of evil you will ever read, this one from so long ago. But it is part of our history, and maybe it helps explain why we feel guilty about the doubts we have. We think they're a hole in the otherwise seamless robe of our faith.

But I think we can leave both the ancient definition of evil and the ancient suspicion of human doubt behind. Neither one works very well for us. Most of us have learned more from our periods of doubt than we ever learned from our certainties.

THURSDAY IN LENT I

Pss 50 * (59, 60) or 19, 46
Deuteronomy 9:23–10:5
Hebrews 4:1–10
John 3:16–21

For God so loved the world that he gave
his only Son, so that everyone who believes in him
may not perish but may have eternal life.

JOHN 3:16

This is the verse born-again Christians hold aloft on a sign at a football game when the television camera pans the audience, or have tattooed on their arms, or wear on a tee shirt. It is not the oldest confession of Christian faith we have—that one appears in 1 Corinthians 15:3–4: "For what I received I passed on to you as of first importance: that Christ died for our sins according to the Scriptures, that he was buried, that he was raised on the third day according to the Scriptures . . . " (NIV).

They are not the same, are they? The later one, John's, is much more about us—what we think, what we believe, what will happen to us if we believe. The earlier one—forty to fifty years earlier—is about Christ. What happened to him. What he did.

In Paul, we see a church just beginning to wrestle with what the resurrection might mean. Just beginning to come to terms with the puzzling fact that some of the Christians have actually died: This was not expected in the early days. Paul and his friends thought the end of the world was coming any day. And then one day yielded to another. Now what? Throughout the period of his letters, we see Paul making this adjustment. We see him doing what we must also do: adjusting his thinking about God in the light of his experience of life.

By the time John is writing, more things are settled. God the Father and God the Son are clearly defined figures with clear roles in our redemption. The cosmic meaning of the Christ event is more important to Jesus in his speaking than the parables and ethical teaching of earlier writings. Jesus commands belief. Our sins make no appearance in John 3:16. The sin that separates us from eternal life is lack of belief, not the catalogue of human sins Paul assumes. That's a big difference.

We can see why the newer of the two is the one they hold up at football games. It is more triumphal. Less ambiguous. Clearer.

Maybe. But it was not the first. We are humbled by the ancientness of Paul's confession of faith, by the very fact of all its loose ends. John 3:16 may fit on a sign better, but 1 Corinthians 15:3–4 sounds more like us.

FRIDAY IN LENT I

Pss 95, 40, 54 * 51
Deuteronomy 10:12–22
Hebrews 4:11–16
John 3:22–36

Indeed, the word of God is living and active, sharper than any two-edged sword, piercing until it divides soul from spirit . . .
HEBREWS 4:12

We are divided, all of us. Those of us who think that is not true of them just have not thought the matter through.

We do things we know will hurt us. We do things we honestly don't want to do. We regret it later, but in a little while, we do them again. *What was I thinking?* we ask ourselves, and we have no good answer. We resolve to do other things, good things for ourselves and others. And the sun sets, and—once again—we have not done them.

Even our good deeds are, in part, performances for an audience. We long for praise and feel hurt if it does not come. We deny this to ourselves and others.

We treat those who love us as if they would always be here. They will not always be here. We know this, but we do not change our ways. We want them to meet our needs. Sometimes we do not remember that the business of meeting needs is always a two-way street.

The word of God is truth. Truth about ourselves and about the world. Truth about hard things. But truth, also, about a wonderful thing—God already knows about our divisions. God was never fooled, even on those occasions when we fooled ourselves. The painful piercing of our hearts by the two-edged sword of God's love is only for our good, only to bring us closer to the oneness we crave. Division maybe our universal lot, but it has never been our destiny.

SATURDAY IN LENT I

Pss 55 * 138, 139:1–17 (18–23)
Deuteronomy 11:18–28
Hebrews 5:1–10
John 4:1–26

*"Sir, give me this water, so that I may never be thirsty
or have to keep coming here to draw water."*
JOHN 4:15

Not terribly spiritual, the Samaritan woman. She's not as interested in religion as she is in shaving a little off her back-breaking
workload.

Life had been hard on her. The work, of course, was hard: She
was the water-bearer of the house, a heavy yoke bearing leather bags,
several trips a day. She usually went very early in the morning,
before it got too hot, but also before her husband needed the water.

Not that he was her husband, really. Life, as I said, had not been
especially kind to her. But she had always found a man to take care
of her, which was more than some poor women with no dowries
and no children were able to do. So it could certainly have been
worse, she supposed. And he wasn't a bad man. He liked his meals
ready for him when he was ready to eat and his bath prepared when
he was ready to take it. He liked his clothes washed before they
needed it and he liked the house clean. He liked fresh eggplant, fresh
eggs, and he liked the way she rubbed his back when it hurt from
working in the quarry, which was mostly every day. Things could
have been much worse.

People, though, were unthinking. Cruel, even. They did not accord
her the status of a wedded wife, of course, and she didn't expect it
from them. But she was not a slave, either. Or a prostitute. The life
they lived was no different from the lives men lived with their wives,
but she was never included in the dinners in the women's quarters
when there was a wedding or a feast. Never once. He would go, and

she would stay home alone. She would hear the laughter and the music from the quiet of his tiny house. That hurt.

The hell with them. She didn't need friends. Her husband was a good man. Not that he was her husband, really.

One friendly word from a stranger. A friendly, nonsexual word. Respectful. From a Jew, of all people. She stopped and gave him a drink.

And her whole life was opened up to her. She was seen clearly, she and her whole people. Everything was clear and none of it got in the way.

She ran all the way back to town.

SUNDAY, LENT II

Pss 24, 29 * 8, 84
Jeremiah 1:1–10
1 Corinthians 3:11–23
Mark 3:31–4:9

"Ah, Lord God! Truly I do not know
how to speak, for I am only a boy."
JEREMIAH 1:6

It's 10:30 at night on the train, and all the commuters who worked late today sit in silence. But they are not the only ones riding tonight: There was a Rangers hockey game, so the train is full of red, white, and blue tee shirts on bodies of all ages and shapes, including those of three little boys, who ride with their mother.

There are other boys on the train, older boys, who also went to the game—men, really. One of them is relating a story to the others, and his language is peppered with curse words. Really bad ones. Words that the three little boys really don't need to hear. Words that I don't need to hear, either, after a long day.

I'm not sure anybody else is listening, though. Not even their mother, who leans against the window and rests her eyes. The little boys had other fish to fry: The littlest, overtired, kept attacking his middle brother, needing to be peeled off him every few minutes. Some kids get physical when they're tired, attempting impossible tasks, inconsolable when they fail at them.

The boys poke at each other, invade each other's space, tell on each other to their mom. *Make him stop hitting me!* the middle one says, socking his brother on the arm.

The men continue their cursing. I guess people don't really hear themselves talk any more. I guess words in general don't mean much, and the power of a curse is just about gone.

The men acted like children. The children fought like mad soldiers. The weary workers slept, and the mother. The train sped on through the night.

MONDAY IN LENT II

Pss 56, 57, (58) * 64, 65
Jeremiah 1:11–19
Romans 1:1–15
John 4:27–42

I am a debtor both to Greeks and to barbarians,
both to the wise and to the foolish . . .
ROMANS 1:14

This is a radical change: We know that Paul has been raised to think exactly the opposite. Up to now, his obligation has been to stay *away* from Greeks and barbarians, and it has been a serious one. He has been something of a religious hall monitor, not above spying on people and snitching on them. He may have had some people arrested. Killed? Maybe. And now, he's the one who must talk his fellow Christians back home—all Jews—into thinking that you don't have to be Jewish to be Christian.

Imagine: There was a time when those two things seemed utterly fused in everyone's mind. It was the great church controversy of its day—like gay marriage is today, or the ordination of women. For many, Christianity was a tiny sect of Judaism. Period.

Paul is a good choice for this work. He knows the Hellenistic world. He speaks Greek well. He is sophisticated.

And there's one other thing: He's crabby. He has a certain flair for alienating people. Paul doesn't mind hurting your feelings if he thinks you're wrong about something he cares about. He succumbs easily to his own competitive instincts where other leaders are concerned, and he's sensitive about his Jewishness, eager for everyone to know just how observant he was. When he was observant. You can tell it's still hard for him to have given up his rigorous purity.

So Paul doesn't mind a good argument, and he rises passionately to his own defense. He is well versed in scripture, well trained in debate, and he loves to write letters. Letters in Greek. This is our good luck. We still read them, plumbing them for universal truths amid his wrangling and his sarcasm. We smile at his bravado and wonder at his courage. Not a perfect man, Paul. But the very man for his calling.

TUESDAY IN LENT II

Pss 61, 62 * 68:1–20 (21–23) 24–36
Jeremiah 2:1–13
Romans 1:16–25
John 4:43–54

What wrong did your ancestors find in me that
they went far from me, and went after worthless
things, and became worthless themselves?
JEREMIAH 2:5

I don't know what I did wrong, she says, hunched over in her chair, as if protecting her stomach from a blow. But no one is here to hit her, not now, not any more than she's already been hit. Her husband has left her. It was sudden, completely unexpected. *But didn't you suspect something was wrong?* her friends ask her. *No,* she says. *I thought we were fine. He was always telling me how beautiful I was, how much he loved me. How lucky he was to be married to me.* They all go home that night and make dinner, put in a load of laundry, wonder what it is to go home and find that you're single and you didn't know it.

Of course, they say to themselves, it takes two to tango. If she didn't see it, it was because she didn't want to see it. But it can't have been true that there was nothing to see.

Yes. But sometimes what there is to see isn't that you did anything so wrong. Sometimes it's just that the other person didn't have what it took to go the distance. Some people are immature. And sometimes, they never do grow up. Sometimes the only mistake you made was getting hooked up with one of these large children in the first place. Sometimes—maybe not for a while—the lady may see that and stop billing herself for someone else's charges.

Isn't it striking: God asks himself the same sad question. *What did I do wrong?* But God already knows the answer—and with God the answer really *is "nothing at all".* Goodness extended to us demands our goodness in return. If we can't return love with love, the consequences belong to us.

WEDNESDAY IN LENT II

Pss 72 * 119:73–96
Jeremiah 3:6–18
Romans 1:28–2:11
John 5:1–18

> *"Sir, I have no one to put me into the pool when the water is stirred up; and while I am making my way, someone else steps down ahead of me."*
>
> JOHN 5:7

The water in the pool was held to be miraculous. Sometimes, people said, an angel came and troubled the water—made it turbulent—and if you could get in the pool when the water was moving, you would be healed.

But there is a hierarchy of the strong over the weak among sick people, too, as there is among everyone else. This man couldn't get to the miraculous pool. Other, stronger people elbowed him out of the way. Time after time, he started his painful way toward the pool. But he never got there. It was the stronger ones, from among that group of the weak, who got healed.

Being weak makes it easy to get weaker. Being poor can make you poorer. Being vulnerable exposes you to greater danger. Criminals look for the weak upon whom to prey: old ladies, disabled people, people who look like they can't fight back. The world hits you when you're down, and it seems to seek those who are down to hit.

This is why Christ comes first to the weak and the poor, to those whom life has hit hard. They are the ones who need him first. He inverts the survival of the fittest, the hard law of life on earth.

Jesus always does this. He is the master of the unexpected: We think we know where the power is, but he inverts power. The way the world works is not necessarily the way God works. A power and a set of values greater than we are govern the larger picture. Over and over, Jesus shows us this power.

THURSDAY IN LENT II

Pss (70), 71 * 74
Jeremiah 4:9–10, 19–28
Romans 2:12–24
John 5:19–29

The hour is coming when all who are in their
graves will hear his voice and will come out . . .
JOHN 5:28–29

This is our dream: They will return to us. It will be as it was before we lost them. We dream of it, sometimes, and those dreams are happy beyond any happiness we have, magic in their happiness. Soaked in joy.

When we awaken, it is a moment or two before we understand that it *was* a dream. *It was so real,* you say to a sleepy spouse, and you go on to tell the dream in as much detail as you can remember. You see, though, that it is not, cannot be, as compelling to anyone else as it was to you. It was your dream. It slips away as you tell it—already you can't summon the whole thing to mind. But you remember the face, the voice you heard. You remember the happiness.

That dream is ours. The biblical dream is different: When the dead hear the voice of the Son of God, a return to this life is no longer important. To them or to us. We are together again, but not in the old way. It is we who will move, not them, into another way of being, something different from what we have now.

Oh, you say, disappointed. *I wanted my dream to be real. I wanted her to come back, like in my dream. I wanted that to be what God does at the end of it all. I wanted that to be the resurrection.*

Many times, in those dreams we sometimes have, the dead one appears to tell us that things are fine. That he is happy. That she is all right. Many dreams of the bereaved contain some version of such reassurance. Wish fulfillment? No doubt. But false, because that is so? Not necessarily.

FRIDAY IN LENT II

Pss 95, 69:1–23 (24–30) 31–38 * 73
Jeremiah 5:1–9
Romans 2:25–3:18
John 5:30–47

What if some were unfaithful? Will their
faithlessness nullify the faithfulness of God?

ROMANS 3:3

Four thousand American priests accused of molesting children
this week. Some of them, no doubt, are innocent. But some are
guilty. People raised from childhood to respect the clergy are
shaken to the soles of their feet. *The priest was God to me*, one man
told a reporter. *It never occurred to me not to do anything he told me
to do. Never.*

But the priest was never God. All of us are to point to God, not
to ourselves. We try to bring the love of God into people's lives, but
priests are not God themselves. It was never a good idea to elevate
them above other human beings. To regard them as superhuman
and to expect them to be superhuman.

Jesus comes to redeem the world, to redeem all human life,
including the mystery of sexual relating. It was never a good idea to
suggest that this mystery had nothing to do with religion, or worse,
that it was opposed to faith. There is a way of health and life where
sex is concerned, and there is a way of death.

SATURDAY IN LENT II

Pss 75, 76 * 23, 27
Jeremiah 5:20–31
Romans 3:19–31
John 7:1–13

*For there is no distinction, since all have
sinned and fall short of the glory of God;
they are now justified by his grace as a gift . . .*
ROMANS 3:22–24

Don't read a meaningless relativism into this. Of course all actions are not the same, nor are they equally laudable or sinful. Paul is not saying that we have no right to distinguish between capital murder on the one hand and using the wrong fork at dinner on the other, or that God doesn't care what human beings do. Of course there are gradations in sin.

But he *is* saying that none of us are without it. That we've all got something to work on. That those who think otherwise must have not looked inward recently and probably should.

For our sins—even the worst of them—do not keep us from the power of repentance and the return to God's love it offers. Only our smugness can do that. If I don't think I need any help, I am unlikely to ask for any. If I don't think I've done anything wrong, I won't seek forgiveness.

This is not really a passage about ethics. It's a passage about the human relationship with God. We still must make hard choices about how we will behave. But we can be sure of a welcome, even when we fall grievously short of where we know we should be. Even if we're not sure exactly where that is.

We don't earn our way into the divine love. We're already there. Ethical challenges abound in all of our lives, and living in God's love usually doesn't simplify them.

SUNDAY, LENT III

Pss 93, 96 * 34
Jeremiah 6:9–15
1 Corinthians 6:12–20
Mark 5:1–20

"All things are lawful for me," but not all things are beneficial. "All things are lawful for me," but I will not be dominated by anything.
1 CORINTHIANS 6:12

I'll leave you this number, but please don't leave a message on it. I don't know how to pick up messages on my cell phone. How embarrassing.

Or how to program my VCR. Or how to play DVDs on my computer. The rumor is that you can do that. I'm not absolutely certain that I know what a DVD is. I don't even know how to cancel the alarm function on my clock radio. It goes on every afternoon at three o'clock.

We're so connected these days, but only if we make it our business to know all about our electronic gadgets. A little knowledge is a very dangerous thing. I have all these conveniences, but only the most rudimentary idea of how to use any of them. The result is that a person could leave me an important cell phone message with confidence that I would receive it, and I would never know. Just thinking about it makes me tired.

Communication is so fast. It was not always so. It took months for a letter to reach its intended reader in Paul's time. First Corinthians, for instance, isn't really 1 Corinthians—there was another letter from Paul to the Christians in Corinth before that one was written. We know this because it is quoted in the one we have. The quoted material above is from that letter, reproduced in what we know as 1 Corinthians, so that Paul could argue with them on the basis of what they had said.

It was a lot of work, staying in touch. Words on paper were hard to come by, and people didn't waste them. Whole communities must have waited eagerly for these letters. Must have set out immediately to copy them out by hand. Memorized them, maybe.

There were many, many writings from the early church that have not survived. Some were rejected when the canon of the New Testament was established, a very political process, and these are read only by scholars today. Most of them have disappeared.

The volume of words today is beyond the ancient imagination. So many words that words themselves have become cheap. Their veracity cannot be assumed or even expected—anyone can set up a blog on the Internet and put out anything at all. It doesn't have to be true. Increasingly, there's no way to tell. Except the old way. Talk about it with people you trust. Test it. Try it and see if it works. Ask yourself if it's in accord with what you know about the way the world functions. And if it sounds too good to be true, it probably is.

MONDAY IN LENT III

Pss 80 * 77, (79)
Jeremiah 7:1–15
Romans 4:1–12
John 7:14–36

"Where does this man intend to go that we will not find him? Does he intend to go to the Dispersion among the Greeks and teach the Greeks?"

JOHN 7:35

Greeks, now. Foreigners. At once we are far from Palestine, far from the first century or from any other century, before or since. This is what the adventure is like from Christ's point of view.

The mortals do not hear us. Or see us clearly. And yet we persist. Here and there, someone notices; here and there, we make ourselves heard. Some can receive us, we think. Maybe more will. There is only one way to find out.

We see that they are not able to bear the weight of the law on their own. This is a tragedy, for the law might keep them from killing each other. But we must face the fact that they cannot lift it and sustain its burden. They can't follow it. We will have to go and bring them to us in another way.

Who shall go? The Source of all Being, upon whom no human can look with honesty and live? Too dangerous for them. The Spirit, whose flutter is so gentle most of them don't even notice her? No. She must have a house built for her there first, a place to contain her gentleness and her power. A place to stay in their midst for ever.

So it will be the Word who will incarnate, that face of God that shapes the raw stuff of Being into the multiplicity of forms that can live on the earth. The one who understands them all best. The Word will be able to live as they live. He will be like them, will stride power-fully along their roads, will stop at their houses. He will sit at table with them. He will be knowable. They will be able to talk to him. He will gather others around him, people who can also talk to them. He will gather men and women, so that men and women can always find someone to whom they can share their hearts. He will even gather children, so that they are part of it all from the moment they are first aware of being part of anything.

It will not work perfectly. Nothing there is perfect. Mostly, they will fight about who is in and who is out. Why do they love so to fight about this? It must be their fear of losing our love, because of all the love they have known and lost. They will give over extraordinary amounts of energy to these arguments. Excluding people from our grace will be the central focus of faith for many of them. This, too, is a tragedy.

But some of them—many of them—will feel the presence of the Word. They will turn from their divisions and recognize the voice. In unguarded moments, they will realize where it all comes from.

TUESDAY IN LENT III

Ps 78:1–39 * 78:40–72
Jeremiah 7:21–34
Romans 4:13–25
John 7:37–52

And they go on building the high place of Topheth . . .
to burn their sons and their daughters in the fire—which
I did not command, nor did it come into my mind.

JEREMIAH 7:31

T he peoples who lived around Israel practiced human sacrifice—some of them, at some times. From this passage, and others like it, it is evident that the children of Israel themselves were
tempted to do the same. In the terrible story of Abraham's near-
sacrifice of his son Isaac by burning him on an altar, we see another
clue. More than once, the children of Israel thought that maybe
their God, too, required this kind of propitiation. And sometime
they gave it to him.

Barbaric, we say, and so it is. The sacrifice of children, prisoners,
servants—we have found this in the history of many ancient soci-
eties. We hate to think that it is in ours, too.

And it probably is. But so is the urgent condemnation of it. *Stop!*
the prophets say. *This practice is not of God. No matter what others
may do, you do not do this.* Abraham begins to relate to God as if
God required his only son at his hand, and God stops him. *I am not
like this. I am not Moloch, or any of the other bloodthirsty gods of your
neighbors. I am yours and you are mine, and the sign of this shall be
human righteousness, not human blood.*

And so, did understanding this about God inaugurate a permanent commitment to nonviolence among Jews, and later among
Christians? No. We continued to shed children's blood in other
ways, and other people's blood as well. We do it today. We continued to imagine that faith in God sometimes takes the form of vio-
lence. We imagine it still. But it never does.

There is still ample room for improvement among us. We still don't get it about God, not entirely. But God gets it about us, and corrects us, as often as we need correcting.

WEDNESDAY IN LENT III

Pss 119:97–120 * 81, 82
Jeremiah 8:18–9:6
Romans 5:1–11
John 8:12–20

And not only that, but we also boast in our sufferings, knowing that suffering produces endurance, and endurance produces character, and character produces hope, and hope does not disappoint us . . .
ROMANS 5:3–5

The voters have rendered their verdict, and I accept it, Joe Lieberman said this morning, pulling out of the Democratic primary competition. He is the third candidate to have done that during this phase of the process. Out of money and out of momentum, they must set aside a powerful dream, and they must do it in public. A sobering occupational hazard of politics.

I just about had my bags packed, a colleague says ruefully. She had been certain the interview at a prospective parish went well, could feel the mutual falling in love she had felt before. But they called someone else.

I gave a good audition, but I just wasn't right for the part, an actor tells me. This happens to him about three times a week. Sometimes more. If there is a profession that buffets the ego more than acting, I don't know what it is. It is not for sissies.

Somebody's got to lose if someone else wins. Most top spots can't be shared. More than anything else, it is fear of losing that prevents us from trying. *People will see me fail. I will become pitiable.*

People are so brave. They try, when they don't know in advance that they will succeed. They try even when they've lost before. They know themselves and they trust their gifts and they believe in them, and so they try again.

It may hurt, but there is no shame in failing. Some of us won't even use the word "failure": It has become a forbidden word in the universe of 24/7 cheer in which we're all supposed to live. You're not allowed to say "failed" and "failure." You're supposed to say something upbeat like "challenge" or "opportunity" instead. But I say there's nothing wrong with failing honestly. I say that a failure doesn't sum up my life, but it's a dandy way to describe the end of a particular hope. I may have a failure—and I have had many—but that doesn't mean I am one. I might hurt because I failed, but I need never be ashamed of it. I can be proud of having gone all out, of having been brave enough to try and fail.

THURSDAY IN LENT III

Pss (83) or 42, 43 * 85, 86
Jeremiah 10:11–24
Romans 5:12–21
John 8:21–32

Woe is me because of my hurt! My wound is severe!
JEREMIAH 10:19

You look like the Phantom of the Opera, I tell Q. He was standing on a chair to get at a piece of metal flashing that had come loose, and the chair tipped, simultaneously spilling him onto the floor and shooting a chair leg directly at his left eye. Now it is a brilliant deep purple with red accents—exactly like our house—and the center of his upper lip is three times its normal size.

Does it hurt? I ask.

No, he says. *Not yet, anyway*. He had taken himself off to the emergency room, since I wasn't at home, and returned five hours later to a wife who was wondering where he was, what the trail of blood leading from the front door back to the kitchen and out the back door might mean. *I had an accident,* he had said on the answering machine. *It's not serious.* Okay.

Another half inch and he would have lost the eye. An inch to the left and he would have broken his nose. Q's face is lurid, all right, but he has remarked several times that it could have been much worse.

Odd—so many things could be so much worse, but few people are as philosophical about their woes as Q is. *My headaches are so worse than other people's,* wrote Jane Austen slyly. The pebble in my shoe or the pain in my tooth occupies my attention, and it can be hard to rise above it.

Misfortune can either instruct us or it can barricade us from the possibility of being instructed. Some of us are compassionate in direct and graceful proportion to the pain we have known in life. And some of us can only refuse the pain of others in order to focus on our own.

How God acts toward pain is clear: The coming of Christ embraces all of it. We are understood by Christ because Christ has lived our life and died our death. God actually knows what it's like to suffer pain and loss. Knows about it the same way we know about it: from personal experience.

And that's what we need. Of course we want all our pain to disappear, but we already know that doesn't happen. Everybody gets some. Since it usually doesn't disappear magically, we could all use some understanding of its effect on us. And that's what we have in Christ. From personal experience.

FRIDAY IN LENT III

Pss 95, 88 * 91, 92
Jeremiah 11:1–8,14–20
Romans 6:1–11
John 8:33–47

"Whoever is from God hears the words of God. The reason
you do not hear them is that you are not from God."
JOHN 8:47

There were lots of kids in the museum with us, lots of kids, and adults feeling like kids, for a few moments: looking at the dinosaur footprints in solid rock, trying to figure out what the animal was doing. Walking? Running? Just sitting there, looking around? Drinking from a pool of water? Dying?

One family with three kids swarmed along through the dino tracks and out into the rest of the museum, to an impressive group of dino skeletons. The kids walked along a wall detailing the progression of early hominids, looking at the sloping skulls and reading about them. Their mother walked anxiously behind them.

Samantha, I think I see a great lesson for Sunday school! she said enthusiastically, pointing away from the hominids to a mammoth with six-foot tusks. *God made each one with everything it needed to live. Look at those big tusks!*

Hey, look at this one! her little boy said. It was Australopithecus. *It's twenty-five million years old!*

Well, Mommy doesn't believe that, she said. I studied a nearby Neanderthal and listened. *Those aren't really early human beings. They were animals domesticated by people, like apes. Mommy believes that God made us just as we are, just like that.*

Well, did they have the dinosaurs as pets, then? her daughter asked.

Um . . . I think they probably did, said the mother doubtfully. *Ooh, look at those birds over there!*

But it says . . . the little boy protested, looking more closely at the explanation.

Mommy doesn't believe that, she said again, sounding harried. Poor Mommy. So bound to the letter of the Book that the God the Book reveals seemed bound, too. But God is not bound. God is free. Fill the earth, and subdue it. Understand it. Become, yourselves, as free as someone who is not God can be. And grow in wisdom, more and more. Never try to go back. You can't go back. I have placed you in history, and history only moves forward. Be brave enough to move forward with it. And I will be with you always, as I was at its beginning, even to its end.

SATURDAY IN LENT III

Pss 87, 90 * 136
Jeremiah 13:1–11
Romans 6:12–23
John 8:47–59

But now the loincloth was ruined; it was good for nothing . . . Just so I will ruin the pride of Judah and the great pride of Jerusalem.
JEREMIAH 13:7, 9

Well, there's a novel teaching tool: I will make your pride like a dirty pair of underwear.

We forget just how earthy our forbears were. We certainly don't want anybody to do anything impolite in church, or to be insufficiently well groomed. People should behave themselves, shouldn't be loud, or distracting in any way. This particular passage from Jeremiah is not part of the three-year lectionary read at Sunday celebrations of the Eucharist—you're only going to encounter it in worship at morning or evening prayer. Just as well—can you imagine the giggles that would spread through the congregation, once people realized that the Bible reading was about underwear?

You have to wonder—did Jeremiah really do this? And what did the people say, when he held up his dirty underwear and told them it reminded him of them?

And the underwear motif continues: "For as the waistcloth clings to the loins of a man, so I made the whole house of Israel and the whole house of Judah cling to me" (Jeremiah 13:10). Okay. We fit together, God and us, like well-fitting underwear. Somehow that feels like more than we needed to know.

You can't choose your relatives. The people in the Bible just were what they were, and we must accept them as they were, and not try to dress them up and make them presentable. Early in the church's history, there were those who really just couldn't see the point of doing this and wanted the Christian scriptures to eliminate the Hebrew ones. The Old Testament was too coarse, too earthy. Too violent. And it is all those things.

So we need not be like them. But it would be a bad idea to forget them.

SUNDAY, LENT IV

Pss 66, 67 * 19, 46
Jeremiah 14:1–9, 17–22
Galatians 4:21–5:1
Mark 8:11–21

We look for peace, but find no good; for a time
of healing, but there is terror instead.
JEREMIAH 14:19

There is news of P———. He has been arrested for spraying parked SUVs with red paint while riding a bicycle along a street on the Upper West Side. Oh, dear.

Well, that's P———. He has been this way ever since returning from Vietnam, where he saw and did some things that have haunted him for thirty-five years. Mostly the haunting sends him to places more hazardous than West End Avenue. He is on a plane as soon as he hears of trouble, to Northern Ireland, Somalia, Bosnia, Rwanda, Kosovo, Iraq. Once he infiltrated a right-wing militia group in New

York City. You probably didn't know we had right-wing militia groups here, but you can get anything in New York. He goes with press credentials sometimes, and sometimes he goes without. Sometimes he goes to make a documentary film. He uses a digital camera I bought him years ago, when I had money.

So P—— reports on the news, and sometimes he makes a little news himself. I haven't seen any stories about the blood on the SUVs yet, thank God. I don't know why I should feel protective of P——, obviously a man who can take care of himself, but I do. There is an ethical purity about him that I want preserved from harm. P——'s unique combination of journalism and self-destruction doesn't make this easy. I wish he would stop doing things like this. *Grow up, P——,* I scold him in my mind. But P—— is already grown up. He grew up suddenly, at nineteen, when he saw and did whatever it was that he saw and did.

Such people come along once in a while. They do illegal things, sometimes, and sometimes they go to jail. Jesus did some illegal things. Dr. King spent a lot of time in jail. So did Gandhi. So did Nelson Mandela. Not everybody in jail is a criminal. Not everybody isn't. Some of them are a little of both.

P—— would snort at sharing the same paragraph with Dr. King or Gandhi, and it is true it is his imprisonment that is what he has most in common with them. His sorrow is more savage than theirs. P—— is not what Hindus would call a *mahatma,* a "great soul." He is a tortured one, roaming the earth in perpetual atonement for all its terrors.

When he comes home from one of his tours of hell, P—— has a routine. He has coffee with friends. He goes to meetings. He writes and edits film and looks for more work.

And he does one other thing. He goes to a hospital and sits in a rocking chair, where he cuddles and rocks the babies who live there. He once told me that the time he spends holding the babies is the only time he feels at peace.

Lord, have mercy.

MONDAY IN LENT IV

Pss 89:1–18 * 89:19–52
Jeremiah 16:10–21
Romans 7:1–12
John 6:1–15

"There is a boy here who has five barley loaves and two
fish. But what are they among so many people?"
JOHN 6:9

I never did divide and move all the irises. Last fall, I learned just in time that a group of scented geraniums I thought hardy in our climatic zone were not, so they all had to come in. Now geraniums outnumber us inside the house by about ten to one. I did bring the dahlia tubers in. I was reminded of them this morning, talking to Anna on the phone. She's at our house.

"What are those things in the bottom of the refrigerator? Beets?" I couldn't place what she was talking about. "You know, in the bottom? Wrapped in a paper towel—they look like turds?"

"Oh, the dahlias." I hadn't thought of them as turdlike, but actually . . . well, never mind. I had to take them out of the ground early, and gave them an artificial winter in the icebox. I had forgotten they were there. All the rest of the dahlias are biding their time down in the basement.

I was still laughing at the turds when we hung up. I guess a dahlia tuber is truly an ugly thing, at that. It is never finished, a garden, until the winter covers it with a blanket of snow. And even then, you're thinking about it. They start sending you seed catalogues when everything is still brown and frozen, and you begin to feel spring budding in your heart again, months before it buds anywhere else.

Many things start invisibly like that. Babies do: They are too small to see when they come into being, tiny cells, unknown to anybody, even to their mothers. And they grow, until their presence is obvious to everyone, and then they appear, round and downy as a peach. Love starts that way, too, usually: not a sudden blast of passion, but a warming of the heart, felt before you name it, surprising you with its gradual grace. Forgiveness starts silently, invisibly, too. You won't and won't forgive for years—and then you begin to pray in earnest to be delivered from the burden of hating someone else and gradually your enemy takes human form in your imagination again, and you begin to know freedom again.

There is always more afoot than we know. God has thoughts beyond ours and acts beyond our acting. No woman gets herself pregnant, no plant grows itself, no one falls in love by himself, no one possesses within herself the power to forgive. All of us who act are also acted upon by the Spirit of God that gives us all life, and our strength is never all the strength there is.

TUESDAY IN LENT IV

Pss 97, 99, (100) * 94, (95)
Jeremiah 17:19–27
Romans 7:13–25
John 6:16–27

Yet they did not listen or incline their ear; they stiffened
their necks and would not hear or receive instruction.
JEREMIAH 17:23

Crossing the street, I study the pavement as I near the curb: I know that the rapids will be narrower in one spot than in others, narrow enough to step across, and I must find that spot. Why that is, I do not know, but it is true at almost every corner: You can usually find a narrow place over which to hop back up onto the sidewalk.

The water is fast as it heads toward the grate. It carries everything with it, and it soon overwhelms the capacity of the pipes below the street to receive it, so that water flows forwards and backwards at once around the openings. It carries all the litter people throw in the New York streets down, down, and then carries it a distance, so that it appears on the beach in New Jersey next summer. That's why you found a hypodermic needle on the beach: not because people are shooting up there, but because people are shooting up *here*. Truth: Beach litter comes primarily from the city street. It commutes, like everybody else.

All the beautiful things are one, and all the unlovely things are one, as well. The same one. Nothing happens alone. Everything affects everything else. There isn't just an ecology of the natural world—there's an ecology of everything.

We don't really believe this. We take our strong sense of self and project it onto the world, convincing ourselves that we are really separate and autonomous. We lean against the piano and sing "I Gotta Be Me," and feel courageous. This must be what integrity is, we think as we sing: not letting anybody tell me what to do. This must be it.

But that is not what integrity is. That is something else. Self-absorption, I think.

Integrity is being brave enough to see my actions clearly, in all their implications. The implications for me, yes, but also for the ones whose lives they will affect. Integrity is being brave enough and honest enough to accept the ecology of my actions, and not try to explain it away in either a stammer or a bellow of self-justification. Integrity is knowing that there really is no such thing as a free lunch, not here on earth. Heaven is a glorious banquet, absolutely free, but down here, you pay.

WEDNESDAY IN LENT IV

Pss 101, 109:1–4 (5–19) 20–30 * 119:121–144
Jeremiah 18:1–11
Romans 8:1–11
John 6:27–40

*"Do not work for the food that perishes, but for
the food that endures for eternal life . . . "*
JOHN 6:27

"Wait a minute," I told Norah. "I need to give you some pie before you leave."

I made two pies the other day: one with the last of the frozen rhubarb from the garden and an apple pie. Like a spawning salmon swimming desperately upstream, I have an inner switch that something in the arrival of autumn trips: Autumn makes me want to bake pies, and I continue baking them all winter long. Lots of pies. I bake three, at least, for Thanksgiving. And I bake warm-up pumpkin pies beforehand. Pies for the Christmas Fair across the street. *Tartes tatins*, displayed on lace paper doilies that I hope look French for Valentine's Day. Lemon tarts. Pecan pies. Pies with different kinds of crusts, just to try them.

Here is the thing about pies, though: in order not to utterly cancel out all my good work pushing and pulling and gyrating at the gym, I can't just go home and eat a pie. So I have a rule: I can eat a piece of pie. That's it. But Q can't eat a whole pie, either.

This means that people who come to our house sometimes have to leave it with pie. It's best if I get rid of about half, including the one piece that is my honorarium for baking the pie. "That looks wonderful," Norah says, as I cut off a quarter of a ten-inch apple pie. "That's an awful lot, though."

"We have no choice," I answer firmly, slipping it into a recycled foil pan and shoving it at her. "It can't stay here."

Sometimes I think that the foods to which we are addicted are only stand-ins for the fellowship we love and crave. Our earliest relating revolves around food—in infancy. We enjoy the material gifts of life first in the company of someone we love. Even after she is gone forever, we can have a taste that reminds us of when she was here. "Comfort food," we call it.

But what if we went straight for the comfort instead? What if we just delight in the very making of a pie, in the giving of it? What if we delight in the sharing of tea and laughter? Mightn't we emerge with such satisfaction that we won't really mind not having had the pie that might have gone with it? What if we call someone we love and have a sweet talk instead of a sweet roll? Or a lovely scented bath with a favorite radio show, instead of a candy bar or a martini? What if it turns out that the things we put in our mouths are all substitutes for the love that is our foretaste of the household of God? What if we could go directly to that love, instead of stopping in first with them?

THURSDAY IN LENT IV

Pss 69:1–23 (24–30) 31–38 * 73
Jeremiah 22:13–23
Romans 8:12–27
John 6:41–51

We know that the whole creation has been groaning in labor pains until now; and not only the creation, but we ourselves . . .
ROMANS 8:22–23

The budding of a tree is a more violent process than we think. We are so excited about spring coming that we don't notice how painful the buds of leaves can look at first. They poke their way through the carapace of bark that covers and protects the branch. They swell under the bark, which thins and softens in response to the pressure. They create blisters on the branch, stretched tight to contain the growing bud within. And then they burst through it. Sometimes they are red as blood, inflamed-looking. They line each branch, and we look up at them and see them as almost flowers. Then they, too, are forced off the branch by the green leaf-bundle underneath them, and for a few days the gutters are full of red buds. And then the growing season begins: bright, light green leaves unfurl at last, bearing within themselves the pattern of growth and darkening, set to grow larger and turn a deeper green, breathing in water and air and giving growth, until the time comes for them to burst into one last spasm of brilliance and then drop to the ground in their fiery death.

Oh, the beginnings and endings of things! If we knew how fierce it all was, we would never make a start. Our mothers' wombs would be crowded with babies unwilling to leave, our gardens with seed unwilling to burst apart and set free the tiny green within. And so we are kept in ignorance, and in the valor with which only ignorance can endow us, we stride forth. We don't learn the truth until it's too late to turn back.

Paul compares the whole thing to the urgent pain of childbirth. Don't be afraid, Christ says, fearsome as it all is. There is a hand guiding you. Your progress is certain if you keep walking, for you do not walk alone. Many have made this walk; look to their experience and learn from it. I have made this walk; trust me.

FRIDAY IN LENT IV

Pss 95, 102 * 107:1–32
Jeremiah 23:1–8
Romans 8:28–39
John 6:52–59

For I am convinced that neither death, nor life, . . . will be able to separate us from the love of God in Christ Jesus our Lord.
ROMANS 8:38, 39

The Ice Man is the world's oldest mummy—5,000 years old, or more. He's unusual: His clothing was preserved, as were his last meal and even his quiver of arrows. He is very fragile, and they don't want to break him, so examining him has been a slow process.

But they've found traces of four different people's blood on his clothing, and they've determined that he was shot in the back with an arrow. So he didn't go down without a fight, and, in the end, it took a coward to kill him. He wasn't always fragile.

We're fascinated with these occasional finds: the bog men, the little Inca sacrificial victims, the Ice Man. People who stand at the brink of death and are transfixed there, in our imaginations, caught forever. They aren't caught forever, of course. Their souls went on, like all souls. It is the presence of their intact bodies that arrests our attention and their still-visible suffering. They bring us close in our imaginations to that moment at the end of our own lives, that moment we hardly dare contemplate.

In the imaginations of the living, the dead are frozen in their agony. If we have loved them, this haunts us, waking and sleeping. It is as if the last moment of life were a moment that goes on forever. But it does not go on. It is over now. They are not there any more. The body that once housed his spirit is now an object. It cannot be further injured. Wound it, and it will not bleed. It will never bleed again. Only the living bleed.

I do not know what it is like not to believe that life continues after the short span of life on the earth. Ignorant as I am about what it will be like in an existence in which there is no time, a life not tied to matter and its maintenance, I do not know what it is like to believe that there is no such life. That there is only nothing. I don't believe there can be such a thing as nothing. That there are no automobiles or eyelashes, that there are no smiles and no apples, that seeing and tasting and feeling do not follow us there: This I can believe, although my imagination fails to encompass it. But not nothing.

Where is the Ice Man? Where are all the little Incas, taken so cruelly from their mothers and killed as ritual sacrifices? And where are those grieving mothers, and whatever happened to their broken hearts? All that is over for them. We have their bodies, and gaze upon them in mingled curiosity and fear. But they themselves are long gone. They live in another place that is not a place at all. Their sorrow is over. Ours continues, connected by every sinew to all our earthly joys.

No wonder we do not understand.

SATURDAY IN LENT IV

Pss 107:33–43; 108:1–6 (7–13) * 33
Jeremiah 23:9–15
Romans 9:1–18
John 6:60–71

*For I could wish that I myself were accursed and cut
off from Christ for the sake of my own people . . .*
ROMANS 9:3

We have come a long way from this statement. For many, many people, Christianity is unrecognizable if it is not all about me and whether I am saved. About my well-being and my serenity and my inner life and my Jesus and well, just *me*. And now here is Paul saying, almost as an aside, that he would give up his salvation completely for the sake of his fellow Jews. That their well being was more important than his own good.

Here is the dilemma: Is our Christian faith only instrumentally valuable? That is, is it a way for us to be healthier? Like vitamin pills and exercise and regular checkups? Is it really all about us?

Because if it is, then there are a few things that will have to go.

Like martyrdom. Not just sick no-no-never-mind-I'll-just-sit-here-and-suffer martyrdom, but the real thing. If your own life is the highest good, then you're never going to sacrifice it for that of another. No matter whose. No matter what.

Like a fair amount of human ethics. Don't do anything or feel anything or watch anything or listen to anything that upsets you. Don't let yourself get angry. Don't worry about anything. Don't listen to the news. Don't go where you might get a germ or miss a meal or have a bad feeling.

Like the cross. The crucifixion was not a good career move. Jesus lost his serenity there a couple of times. If Christianity is all about serenity, then the cross is out.

This begins to feel more and more bankrupt the more I think about it. Our faith can't be just about our own mental and physical health and emotional state of well being. It must be about something beyond ourselves, or it cannot be our faith. There must be an *other* in which we place our hope and love and trust. It must place demands on us, demand that we grow into its goodness. It must pull us into becoming more like it. God must be and do these things, or God is not God.

SUNDAY, LENT V

Pss 118 * 145
Jeremiah 23:16–32
1 Corinthians 9:19–27
Mark 8:31–9:1

For those who want to save their life will lose it . . .

MARK 8:35

Victor Schramm was funny, handsome, and brilliant. Of his generation of Episcopal priests, one of the best; a rising star. His setting of the vesper hymn *Phos hilaron* remains the most beautiful one the Church possesses. When I am singing Evening Prayer all by myself, his is the one I sing.

Victor was struck by a garbage truck while standing on a New York City street corner. He died instantly. Every time I see one of the huge white trucks bearing down on me, I think of him. How easy it is to extinguish even the brightest human light. It just takes a second of being in the wrong place at the wrong time.

We are so fragile. A breath of wind can blow us away forever. We haven't much time.

And so, two things: (1) hold this life lightly and (2) make it count. Don't think you have all the time in the world. You don't. Don't allow a moment of whatever time you do have to be spent in bitterness or despair. Or, worst of all, in apathy.

And another thing. Don't be so afraid of dying that you forget to live. There is no telling how many other beautiful things Victor would have written had he survived. How many books he would have written. He would have become a bishop, for sure, and he would have been an ornament to that order.

But his life was complete in the time allotted to it. He used it well. More than that, the oldest among us cannot do.

MONDAY IN LENT V

Pss 31 * 35
Jeremiah 24:1–10
Romans 9:19–33
John 9:1–17

"Who sinned, this man or his parents, that he was born blind?"
JOHN 9:2

I hope you have a daughter just like you, my mother snarled at me, once when I was being difficult. This was not, I could tell, a blessing on my future fertility. Nope—it was a curse. *May the hard time I'm having settle, in the very same way, upon the one who's making it hard.*

What goes around, comes around, we tell each other ominously, when we see someone getting away with murder. He'll get his. We expect a symmetry between offense and punishment, and we tell each other that there is one.

But there isn't. People's actions do have consequences, but they aren't necessarily the moments of elegant justice and deserved comeuppance we think they should be.

I didn't have a daughter just like me. My daughters were just like themselves. They gave me some of the grief I gave my mother, but not all of it. And they made up some grief of their own, too. Some of the things I did well, they didn't do at all, and some of the things I cannot do are some of the things they do best.

I felt an irrational fear, sometimes, that I would be punished through them for all my youthful mistakes. That every misstep I made as a mother would prove to be the decisive one, the deal breaker, that terrible point after which you can never make it right again. That even things I did wrong *before* I became a mother would return to haunt them. That there was something epic about my errors; something immense and biblical. That's a fairly grim load for a young mother to carry. Even now, years later, I can easily summon the dread. I don't care what you've done, nobody in the world has that much power.

Jesus brushes all this morbidity aside. *Nonsense*, he says. *Things don't work like that.* Life isn't like a machine, into which you put the requisite coins and receive the expected prize. We are free, free and alive. The good and the bad that comes into our lives comes in a variety of ways, and we don't orchestrate or cause very many of them. Life is life: It's alive, and one of the things being alive means is that just about anything can happen.

TUESDAY IN LENT V

Pss (120), 121, 122, 123 * 124 125 126, (127)
Jeremiah 25:8–17
Romans 10:1–13
John 9:18–41

"If you were blind, you would not have sin. But now that you say, 'We see,' your sin remains.
JOHN 9:41

A dark day yesterday—the head of the BBC resigned in disgrace. It was a case rather like that at the New York *Times* last year, when a reporter was revealed to have fabricated almost everything he submitted for several months running. His superiors eventually resigned, too, although it took them longer. An American's sense of honor has an extra layer or two of lawyers through which it must pass first.

It's had to say you're sorry, and it's harder here than it is almost anywhere else. We are grimly familiar with the tap dance that follows any important person's indictment: righteously indignant denials on television, with a lawyer constantly at the elbow of the accused. Attempted identification with well-known innocent victims from Jesus Christ on down. If it's an accusation of marital infidelity, the wife is trotted out to stand loyally beside her wronged husband; the grim set of her mouth always seems to me to be as much for her spouse as it is for his accusers. Wait until she gets him home.

When it's time for the trial, he enters the courtroom smiling, as if it were a victory rally. He tells reporters he's confident of being completely cleared. His lawyer reports the plea bargain later on, and her client is nowhere to be seen. In no way is her client is guilty, she assures us. This is just a way to save everybody else a lot of pain. That's the kind of wonderful guy he is. Always thinking of others.

In the end, regardless of the spin, he must admit guilt and pay a price. Why it seems better to string this inevitability out for months or even years and spend millions of dollars doing it had never been clear to me. It's going to be revealed anyhow.

I suppose that's the thing: They never think it's going to be revealed. People always think they're going to get away with what they do. Why doesn't punishment deter crime? Because criminals never think they'll be caught.

Lesser folk like us are like that, too. We didn't do it. We even try to have secrets from God, as if God didn't know what we'd done. Avoid confession, sometimes for years, because we can't bear to say out loud what we know in our hearts. Afraid that, if we say it, God will hear it and know the truth. The good news is that God knows already. Knows what we did and knows why. Knows all about our anxious self-justification. It's not a secret. And it doesn't interrupt the steady flow of the divine love. The sooner you can get to the place of honesty, the sooner God can comfort and sustain you.

WEDNESDAY IN LENT V

Pss 119:145–176 * 128, 129, 130
Jeremiah 25:30–28
Romans 10:14–21
John 10:1–18

I have shown myself to those who did not ask for me.
ROMANS 10:20

The moon shining on ice is different from the moon shining on water: An icy surface is flat, a milky canvas for the moon. Water is deep: It receives the moon and pulls it down into its depths, so that we see it lengthen, moving with the movement of the water. Not so with ice. Ice is still. Nothing moves in ice. The sticks of abandoned finger piers point crazily in a dozen directions, bent by the weight of water trying to drag them away, now that their job is done. A working vessel is a rarity here, these days.

But not all the ships are gone. There is a light on in the window of a small fishing boat as I pass it along the shore: Somebody is aboard. Somebody lives there, I bet, somebody who doesn't mind the tight quarters or the solitude. Somebody who wants to be left alone.

Hear your feet tap along the deck and pull open the heavy door. Step across the raised threshold into the accommodations and fasten the door behind you. It is warm in here. Steam rises from the spout of a coffee pot on the two-burner stove. The tiny table is covered with oilcloth, and it is bolted to the floor. This room is a mess; the occupant doesn't put things away. And so his magazines are in a pile on the bench that will become his bed later on in the evening, and his jacket hangs on the back of the one chair. His radio crackles a song from twenty years ago, and a bowl of chili sits in front of him. Suppertime.

He is surprised at the visit, and not entirely pleased, you can tell, although he greets you politely. There is a reason that his vessel is so small: He is a lonely man by choice. But he accepts the magazines, apologizes for the mess and offers coffee from the pot. You accept with thanks. The coffee is terrible. You talk about the vessel and the business. Inquire after his health and any need he might have. Shopping? Drug store? You make these inquiries offhandedly, without seeming concern. He is not a person who likes to be fussed over. No, he needs nothing. His crewmate comes to the vessel each morning; he has a wife and kids and goes home at night. This man just stays on board. He has no one.

You leave your card. *In case you ever need anything,* you say. *We're here.* You have not mentioned God once in the entire visit, but now you say good-bye and God bless you. Be safe, you say, and he says thank you. And thanks for the magazines. Outside, the moon is high in the black sky, and the frozen shore reflects it dully. Your feet tap along the deck, and you make the long step back over the water to the dock. You car is cold. It starts promptly, though, and you turn on the headlights and begin to drive slowly away from the vessel, jolting along on the pitted ground; there is no road down here. That's about it for today, you think. Time to go home.

THURSDAY IN LENT V

Pss 131, 132, (133) * 140, 142
Jeremiah 26:1–16
Romans 11:1–12
John 10:19–42

Then the officials and all the people said to the priests and the prophets, "This man does not deserve the sentence of death, for he has spoken to us in the name of the Lord our God."
JEREMIAH 26:16

It was the secular people who recognized the voice of God through Jeremiah. The religious leaders didn't get it.

It is our great spiritual danger: We will become so protective of our privilege within our own little world, so content to be protected by the larger one, that we will acquiesce in its evils. That we will buy temporal power we should not have by offering spiritual absolution we should not give. It was possible, on religious grounds, to argue for slavery and against women's rights, and these sorry documents survive. You can read them. It was possible, on religious grounds, to argue for the objectives of the Third Reich, including its genocide. Those texts survive, as well. It is possible to argue, on religious grounds, that the rich have no direct responsibility for the condition of the poor. That illness is a punishment for sin. And that the lives of gay and lesbian individuals and families are an abomination before God.

Scripture is full of words. A clever and determined mind can easily harness them to an evil purpose. A lazy one can drift on them into a place of injustice without even knowing it. So the people of faith need to be smart. Need to think for themselves and accept the gift of reason God has given us all. Won't have the option to avoid learning from history. Must ask themselves what every moral agent must always ask himself: Who benefits from my line of reasoning? Is it I? Or someone powerful, who has my allegiance? And is this as it should be?

FRIDAY IN LENT V

Pss 95, 22 * 141, 143:1–11 (12)
Jeremiah 29:1, 4–13
Romans 11:13–24
John 11:1–27 or 12:1–10

"Lord, if you had been here, my brother would not have died."
JOHN 11:21

The rector across the street is away, so I'm taking his 10:00 healing service. I remember this service from when I was a curate there twenty-three years ago, remember who used to come regularly. Just about all those people have died by now. There is a new crop of the faithful, the fearful and the bewildered on Wednesday mornings now.

It features the Laying On of Hands. That goes all the way back to the New Testament and even further, the idea that prayer for the sick should be accompanied by physical touch. Sometimes just the priest places both hands on the head of the one who seeks healing; in other places, the whole body gathers around and places a hand somewhere, either on the person or on one of the other people praying. It is rather like a football huddle. It is rather like the completing of an electrical circuit. It is rather like both.

Healing comes from God alone. We pray for healing without knowing in advance what will happen, which is what distinguishes prayer from shopping—in shopping, you know what you're going to get, and you can return it if it doesn't suit. Or from ordering from a menu. Or from giving instructions to an employee, or commanding a powerful but obedient genie. Whatever prayer for healing is, it is not a way of ordering God to do our bidding. Or finding a way to talk God out of making people sick. We don't think God makes people sick.

Prayer for healing opens many more mysteries than it solves. In fact, I'm not aware that it solves any mysteries at all. The *why* of sad things remains stubbornly unknowable, the outcome of most things utterly unforeseen. The people gather together, touching each other on the head, on the shoulder, gently, before the God who created them and to whom they will all someday return.

After the Laying On of Hands, they gather again at the table of the Eucharist. Life is hard here, it says silently as they repeat the familiar old prayers, but there is more than just what you see. A larger life awaits us, exists even now, all around us, although we do not see it. They take a sip of wine and a crumb of bread, and it enters their bodies, becomes part of their physicality.

I will hang up my white alb and put my stole away. I will remember the people who used to come to this service all those years ago: the little lady who looked like Helen Hayes, Betty and her daughter, Charles who died alone in his living room. Ed, who came when he got his leukemia diagnosis. All healed now, perfect and joyful and alive. It is good of you to be here, I might tell them. Wonderful to be with you again. Thanks for coming.

SATURDAY IN LENT V

Pss 137:1–6 (7–9), 144 * 42, 43
Jeremiah 31:27–34
Romans 11:25–36
John 11:28–44 or 12:37–50

"Where have you laid him?" They said to him,
"Lord, come and see." Jesus began to weep.

JOHN 11:34–35

Kay is famous in her area—in fact, she's nationally known—for her genius with drying flowers. She grows them and dries them. She does flowers for Williamsburg, where I imagine they know a thing or two about what they want in dried flowers. She has a little room in her big old house, in which that's all she does. In this room, the flowers are remembered forever. They are entombed in silica gel, which sucks the water out of them over a period of weeks, and then they emerge, perfectly shaped and perfectly colored, just the slightest sepia tone to all their brightness. For they are no longer living. It is just their bodies we see. And their bodies are beautiful. But just a little sepia, like an old photograph. Just a little sad. *Here we are*, they say. *Yes, it's us. But we no longer live.*

She reinforces their stems with wire and wraps them in tape, so the stems can be bent to a proper shape for the arrangement in which they will dwell. Tulips, frozen in time, delphinia still almost their original brilliant blue. Complicated dahlias, arranged by color, caught at their peak and stopped forever. Roses in their tight swirls of buds. "I cheat a little on the leaves sometimes," she says. "I paint them just a bit here and there."

To see life arrested in the midst of its greatest beauty—a portrait, a dried flower—is a curious delight. A delight tinged with sadness. The gentle touch of a fingertip on a petal reveals all: It is dry, crisp, not soft and yielding, as it was when it was alive. That was a long time ago.

Some of us will look pretty good after the undertaker finishes with us. Better than we looked when we were alive, some of us. So natural, people will think we should get up, will be unable to believe we're not alive. And they will touch our crossed hands, wanting to feel our soft skin again. But we will not be soft. We will be very hard. And cool.

Oh, I see, they will say to themselves, pulling back their hands from our hardness. *I see.* Our softness is elsewhere now, our physical softness and warmth alive only in memory, our pliable souls gone home, far away from the flower-like beauty that lies so still as people pass by and whisper.

Kay is the custodian of the memory of flowers, the midwife of their ongoing song of the brief life they had in the summer sun. *Come back any time*, she says. I can return, to see summer flowers in the winter, there in that little room in that big house. And then I can step out into the cold air of winter, suck it into my lungs and feel my eyes tear with the shock of it, hear my living feet crunch snow, see diamonds of ice on bare branches, catch the pinking sky as the winter sun slants toward evening.

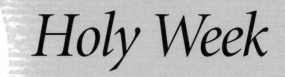

Holy Week

PALM SUNDAY

Pss 24, 29 * 103
Zechariah 9:9–12 * Zechariah 12:9–11; 13:1, 7–9
1 Timothy 6:12–16 * Matthew 21:12–17

Strike the shepherd, that the sheep may be scattered . . .
ZECHARIAH 13:7

"**H**E'S STILL OUT THERE!" screams the *New York Post*. Below the headline, one of the now-familiar pictures of Osama bin Laden. His eyes are surprisingly kind and soft—odd, for we want them to be hard and cruel. Osama uses some of his great wealth to build schools and hospitals, they say. Whatever he doesn't need to fund suicide bombers.

War works best if it's personal. Make it Osama, Hitler, Stalin. Let them stand for their people, and attribute their evil to all the people under their control. Try not to think of the soldier whose rifle is trained on you as a soldier like you. Try not to think of him as human. If you have to kill him, it's better if he never becomes a person in your imagination. If he does become a human being, let him become Osama.

Neither soldier gets out of that encounter uninjured. One is killed or wounded, and the other becomes someone who has taken a life. He can never undo that. You can't unfire your rifle.

And the people at home just pray. For safety, first. *Just let him live.* Try not to think about what might be changing within him. And about his innocence and where it might have gone. There is not a thing they can do about it. *Just let her live. Please. Just let him live.*

As impossible as it seems in a time of war, we also need to pray for those who would do us harm. Our kinship with them is fractured, but it is kinship nonetheless. There will come a time when we will live together in the world as friends; if you doubt this, consider our relationship with Germany and Japan today. The sooner we allow our prayer to glimpse this future, the sooner it will come.

MONDAY IN HOLY WEEK

Pss 51:1–18 (19–20) * 69:1–23
Jeremiah 12:1–16
Philippians 3:1–14
John 12:9–19

Beware of the dogs, beware of the evil workers,
beware of those who mutilate the flesh!
PHILIPPIANS 3:2

"Can Dancer spend the night?" I asked my daughter. Dancer the Dog likes to sleep over.

"We don't have any of her food," Q says. But Dancer had some of the ham from dinner. Just a little. And some of the cats' food, the conquest of which she seems to regard as some kind of victory. The thrill of the chase, I think. In the course of dinner, Dancer went out to pee about seven times: It was a good evening. And later on, after my daughter went home, when Q came back from brushing his teeth, ready for bed, there were three of us waiting for him: me, Kate the cat, and Dancer. Dancer takes up all of Q's side of the bed.

Sleeping with animals: You either like it or you don't. To me, there is nothing better for a chest cold than a nice cat poultice, nothing more soothing for a broken heart than a sigh from a concerned dog. All of our ancient ancestors slept with their newly domesticated dogs and cats, I suppose. Kept them warm at night.

But not the people in the Bible. They didn't like dogs. Didn't keep them as pets, as we do. Dogs in scripture are wild animals that hunted and scavenged in packs. They viewed them as unclean.

We're animals, too, of course. Mammals. Furry, in varying degrees, and warm-blooded. We need one another to keep warm. Highly social mammals, the most social of our phylum: Our young die if they don't have someone to hold them and cuddle them, even if they have enough food and water and are adequately warm. It's not enough. They need company.

The little animals in our lives ask for their dinners. They ask to go outside. They make a mistake and pee on the rug. They get sick and have to go to the vet. The stuff of life unfolds in their short lives, and we accompany them. The people ask for things, too. Harder things. Loving them is more complex. They make mistakes, too, and forgiving them is also more complex.

That's it, we say when a beloved pet dies, I'm never getting another dog. It hurts too much when they die. But later on, a little puffball make his appearance, or a stray cat shows up, and love begins again. Love transforms endlessly, it seems, independently of our assessment of our own capacity to love again. We're better at it than we thought. We have more of it to give than we imagined. Perhaps it is not entirely up to us

TUESDAY IN HOLY WEEK

Pss 6, 12 * 94
Jeremiah 15:10–21
Philippians 3:15–21
John 12:20–26

Very truly, I tell you, unless a grain of wheat falls into the earth and dies, it remains just a single grain; but if it dies, it bears much fruit.
JOHN 12:24

Her mother is ninety-five and she is dying. Mine was sixty-four, and I was still in my twenties. My friend is nearly fifty. So all manner of sensible things apply: She has had her mother in her life for so much longer, her mother has had a long, long life. Her death can't really be considered tragic, not after that long a run.

But sensible things don't count for much at times such as this one. Her eyes fill with tears and her face crumples as she talks about her mom. "Were you expecting your parents' deaths? she asks me. Well, yes, I say, but you're never really ready, no matter how much time you have to prepare. It ought to be easier when the dying one is old, but somehow it's still hard. Not tragic, maybe, but hard nonetheless. We're never ready to say good-bye.

As unnatural a thing as we feel death is, it is really not unnatural at all. It is integral to our lives. We are nourished by the lives of those who leave this world, and they must leave it in order for the generations that succeed them to experience their legacy fully. Each generation must become the elder, must weave its experience into the fabric of history, and then must yield to the next, so that another band of color may enter the tapestry of the world.

We hate it. We can experience death only as an enemy. No matter how reasonable we try to be about it, we can't help but recoil in the face of it. We refuse to speak of it or plan for it, cannot imagine it. We view it as unclean. Many adults have never seen the body of a person who is no longer alive. But the dead are not unclean. They are simply no longer at home. They live a different way now. And the way they live nourishes the way we live, just as the plants are nourished by their spent predecessors.

People whose losses are not so fresh and raw sometimes speak of being nourished or cared for by the beloved dead. She was looking out for me, we might say. Parents sometimes report being cared for by a child, even if the child died at a young age. Sometimes I feel him with me, they say, Sometimes I feel him watching over me. Who is to say? But, at the very least, we can say this: They have made us what we are, all those whom we love but see no longer. We would not be the people we are today if we had not had them in our lives, and if we did not continue to be formed by our love of them.

WEDNESDAY IN HOLY WEEK

Pss 55 * 74
Jeremiah 17:5–10, 14–17
Philippians 4:1–13
John 12:27–36

Cursed are those who trust in mere mortals
and make mere flesh their strength . . .

JEREMIAH 17:5

Sooner or later, we must face facts: There are some rocks we can't lift. They are too heavy for us. Human beings cannot supply all our own needs. We must turn, sometimes, to a power beyond our own.

Well, how do we know there *is* a power beyond our own?

We don't.

We don't know much of anything. We have no proof of anything in the Bible, or of anything else the church has taught.

We don't know the things of faith. We believe them. To believe is to follow, to order our lives in trust. To live in trust.

And so we believe in God, because we have no other help but God. If we are to lift anything at all, we must call on God for help, for the time quickly comes when we are taxed beyond our strength. Then we must ask for more or do without.

Of course, we can do without.

We can remain addicted.

We can remain in a paralyzing state of anger.

We can remain in a state of shame. We don't have to give the heavy load of our sorrows to God. We can hang onto it. We can just stand there, allowing ourselves to be crushed by its weight. We can do that.

But we don't have to.

MAUNDY THURSDAY

Pss 102 * 142, 143
Jeremiah 20:7–11
1 Corinthians 10:14–17; 11:27–32
John 17:1–11 (12–26)

*Because there is one bread, we who are many are
one body, for we all partake of the one bread.*
1 CORINTHIANS 10:17

A moment so lovely I want to comment on it right then and there. I don't, though—we're in the middle of administering communion. But it is lovely, the two voices twining in and out around each other like ribbons of the old words:

> The body of our Lord Jesus Christ, which was given for thee. . . . The blood of our Lord Jesus Christ, which was shed for thee . . . preserve thy body and soul . . . preserve thy body and soul . . . take and eat this . . . everlasting life . . . feed on Him in thy heart . . . drink this in remembrance . . . with thanksgiving . . . and be thankful.

Long, mysterious sentences with archaic cadence, phrases from centuries long past, pronouns not used today, "thee" and "thy." Words that flow slowly and uneventfully into the ears and hearts of some into whose crossed hands I put the thin round wafer of white, or that catch the attention of others unexpectedly: "Preserve thy body and soul unto everlasting life." Everlasting life? Am I being preserved? Kept safe for that life right now, at this moment, with this bread?

Worship can be as deep or as superficial as we make it. There is a place for the superficial in a person's devotional life: those moments when depth eludes us, when we skitter from thought to thought like a bug over the water. At those times, we have done well just to show up. We shouldn't be too hard on ourselves.

Because there will be other times. Times like my moment of awe yesterday morning. Times when words are luminous, familiar objects transformed. Times when time itself stands still. "The body . . . the blood . . . take and eat this . . . drink this . . . and be thankful." For a moment, I thought we might never have to leave the sanctuary. That we might just stay there.

In a way, I am there still.

⟍ GOOD FRIDAY

Pss 95, 22 * 40:1–14 (15–19), 54
Wisdom 1:16–2:1, 12–22 or Genesis 22:1–14
1 Peter 1:10–20
John 13:36–38 * John 19:38–42

The ungodly by their words and deeds summoned death . . .
WISDOM 1:16

I scanned the headlines early this morning. A familiar name caught my eye: Duluth doesn't make the New York *Times* much. And certainly not for this reason: There was a mob lynching of three black men there in 1920.

In *Duluth?* My mother was from Duluth. Duluth is in Minnesota, where everyone is nice and has always been nice. Large and blond and nice. That's what we are in Minnesota.

I remember asking my mother in the 1960s about racial prejudice in Minnesota when she was growing up. She didn't remember any. *We didn't really have any Negroes there*, she said. Well, I guess they had three. And then they had three fewer.

She was five when the lynching happened. Ten thousand people came out to see it. Men had broken into the city jail and hauled the three out. Men? My grandfather was a man and he lived in Duluth. Was he there? Did he go? Did my grandmother go, and did they watch? Did they take my mother? *We didn't really have any Negroes there.*

Impossible. A lynching in Duluth? Where people went ice-fishing and ice-boating, where they built warming-houses on the lake so people wouldn't freeze to death? Where my grandfather grew peonies every summer, checking them anxiously every day the year my parents were married, praying that the peonies would bloom by June 21?

Might they have known? Might they even have seen it? Might they have known it was happening and done nothing to prevent it? There is nobody in my family left to ask. My grandmother told me many stories about Duluth when I was little, but she didn't tell me that one. And now they are all dead. Like the three Negroes who weren't really there.

My kind forebears. My good family. That good city, full of good people. Ordinary people. *Impossible*. But anything is possible for ordinary people. Any goodness, and any evil. They can allow themselves to be led either way. They can visit the church and the killing fields on the same day. They tell themselves that it is their leaders who take them astray, but they are the ones who raise up the leaders, and they are the ones who follow them.

So who killed Christ? Ordinary people. Like you and me. It is not enough to bemoan this evil age. I do not control this age. But I do control myself. Start there.

HOLY SATURDAY

Pss 95, 88 * 27
Job 19:21–27a
Hebrews 4:1–16
Romans 8:1–11

For I know that my Redeemer lives, and that at the last
he will stand upon the earth; and after my skin has been
thus destroyed, then in my flesh shall I see God . . .

JOB 19:25–26

I cannot help but wonder what happened. What was it like, that moment of crossing from death back into life? I have imagined it many times: the heart stirring, the blood beginning to move in the veins again. The science of it fails me immediately, and the scriptures offer little in the way of clues for my wondering: Jesus' post-resurrection appearances are contradictory. It was an event unlike any event. Nothing I know about human life takes me very far toward understanding it.

When I am with someone who has just died, I imagine it. I imagine the engine of life starting up again, the final events of the last few moments reversing themselves. All the working parts are here, I think as I look at the face, the still hands. But the breath of life has gone. Sometimes a person looks as if he could awaken and speak. And sometimes he does not. But I always imagine it.

I have imagined the undoing of the World Trade Center's destruction many times. Imagined the buildings reversing their terrible fall, each floor sliding neatly back into place, all the people and all the copy machines flying back into their offices, settling back into a busy Tuesday morning. While the towers were burning, I looked away from them many times, half thinking that I would not see what I knew I would see when I turned my head back toward them. Even now, I look at a picture postcard I have of the Trade Center at night, all its windows lit. I still can't believe it's really gone.

I wonder if Jesus' friends were like me, imagining the undoing of his death, and wishing for it. I think so; everyone who has known loss has this fantasy. And everyone has had to adjust to another reality. Not that one.

But something else happened to them. Their imagining, while it didn't come true in the way they wished, came true in another way. An inexplicable way. In the dark night, they stirred on their restless beds, sleeping fitfully, dreaming that it had not happened at all, none of it. And then, before dawn, they awoke.